GOD IN THE DEPTHS

Michael Howard is Bishop's Officer for Mission, Ecumenism, and Parish Development in the Diocese of Rochester and has spent 30 years in parish ministry. During this time he has also served as a university and a hospital chaplain, and has helped to train ordinands and evangelists. He is married to Judith and they have three grown-up children. They live in Weald, near Sevenoaks in Kent.

God in the Depths

Images of the Sea in the Development of Faith

Michael Howard

First published in Great Britain in 1999
Society for Promoting Christian Knowledge
Holy Trinity Church
Marylebone Road
London NW1 4DU

British Library Cataloguing-in-Publication Data
A catalogue record for this book is available from the British Library

ISBN 0-281-05172-0

Typeset by David Gregson Associates, Beccles, Suffolk
Printed in Great Britain by Arrowsmiths, Bristol

Contents

	Acknowledgements	vii
	Foreword	ix
	Preface	xi
1	Estonia: faith after the Soviet deluge	1
2	The power of the sea	15
3	Charting the ways of the deep	29
4	The deep in the journey of life	44
5	The Church: bridge over troubled waters?	58
6	Monsters of the deep	72
7	Redeeming the deep	87
8	The tomb and the womb of the deep	102
9	Launching out into the deep	117
	Notes	133
	Index	139

The author and publishers are grateful to the following for permission to reprint extracts:

Jaan Kaplinski, *Through the Forest*, first published in 1996 by The Harvill Press. Copyright © Jaan Kaplinski 1991. Copyright in the English translation © Hildi Hawkins 1996. Reproduced by permission of The Harvill Press.

Jaan Kaplinski, *The Same Sea in Us All*, first published by The Harvill Press in 1990. Copyright © Jaan Kaplinski and Sam Hamill 1985. Reproduced by permission of Sam Hamill, The Harvill Press, London, and Copper Canyon Press, Port Townsend, Washington.

Marie O'Brien, 'Atlantic Drive', from *Poetry Now 1992 Northern Ireland*, reproduced by permission of the author.

Gerard Manley Hopkins, 'The Wreck of the Deutschland' and 'O Death, Death', from *Selected Poetry*, reproduced by permission of Oxford University Press.

T. S. Eliot, Choruses from 'The Rock' I, VII, X, from *Collected Poems 1909–1962*, reproduced by permission of Faber and Faber Ltd, London, and Harcourt, Brace and Co., Orlando, Florida.

Emily Dickinson, 'Exultation is the going', reprinted by permission of the publishers and the Trustees of Amherst College from *The Poems of Emily Dickinson*, Thomas H. Johnson, ed., Cambridge, Mass.: The Belknap Press of Harvard University Press, Copyright © 1951, 1955, 1979, 1983 by the President and Fellows of Harvard College.

'Prayer over the Water', from *The Book of Alternative Services of the Anglican Church of Canada*. Copyright 1985 by the General Synod of the Anglican Church of Canada. Published by the Anglican Book Centre. Used with permission.

The author and publishers have made every effort to trace copyright holders. However, if any material has been incorrectly acknowledged, we would be pleased to correct this at the earliest opportunity.

Acknowledgements

I am deeply grateful to my Bishop, Michael Nazir-Ali; to Norman Warren, Gordon Oliver of the Rochester diocesan staff and the congregation of St George's Weald, for their kindness and support making it possible for me to spend three months of study leave travelling and writing; to Gustav Piir, Dean of Tallinn, who facilitated my stay in Estonia and to the many friends in the churches there who shared their stories and showed my wife and me such generous hospitality; to Michael Bourdeaux and the staff of Keston College Oxford for their interest and practical help; to the Warden and staff of St Deiniol's library, making their unique facilities available to me; to Robin Keeley of SPCK for his courteous and wise oversight; to Anne Richards at the Board of Mission, who read through the manuscript and made many helpful suggestions, and to Bishop Michael Marshall for his words of commendation. Finally I owe so much to my wife, Judith, who has encouraged me throughout the birth of this book, and has helped me on my own faith journey more than she can ever know.

FOREWORD

In an age when spirituality is the buzz word and is frequently marketed as the 'feel good factor' inviting us to escape from the hard realities of a universe compiled of conflicting and dark forces, here is a timely book in the midst of millennium hysteria which encourages a journey into God, inevitably involving a passage through the deep waters of our human crises.

It is not insignificant that the author's first love was the study of geology and geomorphology, a love which he does not leave behind either in his theological awareness or in his personal journey of faith. Rather, he sees the whole of creation and recreation as an on-going process, and human awareness and experience as being inextricably bound up with that process, together with a God who reveals himself in and through that process – not least in the depths as well as in the heights.

Retaining this image and symbol of the depths, he binds together the biblical, the historical and the experiential to give a multi-dimensional view of Christian discipleship, based not on the idolatry of slick certainties, but rather on a living faith which is prepared to go *through* the deep waters of life with its problems, crises and challenges.

The book is rich in symbolism drawn from artists, poets, and the witness of music as well as the images of science and the created order. All this goes to make up a narrative which is eloquent and diverse in its language and in its power to communicate faith. The author shares with the reader something of his own personal journey of faith – a journey which carried him through the depths of bewilderment and confusion, and all this is related with a sensitivity which will surely encourage other travellers as they *undergo* their journeyings back to 'God in the depths'.

> Praise to the Holiest in the heights
> And in the depths be praise. (Newman)

Bishop Michael Marshall
Assistant Bishop in London, Holy Trinity, Sloane Street

Preface

This book has been a long time in coming. It started with a childhood fascination with volcanoes, the sea and the mighty processes that formed the landscape the way we see it. It was natural that my first love was the study of geology and geomorphology. Then came a period of self-discovery through a time of severe depression in my twenties when I became aware of the unseen forces which made up my personality. It was almost as though the influence of people and circumstances moved tectonic plates within my being, creating moods, revealing unexplored depths, sometimes inhibiting and sometimes inspiring the direction of my life. It was then that I could begin to accept myself the way I was, and be less afraid to make the inner journey of faith through doubt and dark times, as well as in flashes of joy. Music has helped me throughout to express the emotions I felt, which could not be articulated adequately in words.

The third element which brought this book to birth is a love of practical theology. As a child I was frightened of God and found the blood, fire and wrathful language of the Bible terrifying. Like many others, I could identify with Gerard Hughes's 'Good Old Uncle George' picture of the Almighty; a God of whom adults spoke in glowing terms which bore no relation to the grim tyrant you discovered when you actually met him.[1] Here was a God who kept a roaring furnace going in the basement of his antiquated mansion for all those who refused to love him gratefully, who did not read the Bible every day, and were not obedient to his commands. At the same time, I distinctly remember a time in my mid-teens, when I felt a great sense of embarrassment when people referred to Jesus Christ and the Gospel story. It was almost as though well-meaning adults were asking me to take seriously someone who did not belong to the real world at all. When I eventually took a first step of faith, Jesus Christ truly became real and personal for me, but I suspect that to begin with, Christian faith was partly protection against an early visit to Uncle George's basement!

Mercifully the tiniest seed of faith can blossom in the most unpromising of soil, through the grace of God. Over the years I have moved on in my faith journey, but these images influenced by a mixture of fear and unreality from my teenage years still remain. As an evangelist, my passion is that people at every stage in life shall respond to the God who is love, and who I believe is nearer to them than they can possibly imagine, whether they claim to believe or not. As a parish priest listening to their struggles of faith, at a time when 'modern' and 'postmodern' ways of thinking overlap, I find this ambiguous mixture of fear and unreality often appears in our conversations. Many modern adults would like to be rid of God, and they show it by living from day to day as though he never existed at all. He is part of the mythology of childhood that all healthy grown-ups are supposed to outgrow. But, come a personal crisis when life, and particularly feelings, for a moment seem out of control, and thoughts turn to him. God won't lie down and we need to discover why.

I believe that one clue lies in the symbolism of the deep, part of the poetry of the Bible story, from first book to last. Here, the depths are always present as part of creation, world history and human experience. Dark and mysterious, sometimes fearful, sometimes fascinating, the deep represents part of the very stuff from which the world was made, undergirding all we are, and all we do, for this is not just Bible imagery. The deep is a suggestive and common way of describing our experience of life, particularly in its problems, crises and challenges.

Is it possible then to find God 'in the depths'? Some excellent books have been written around this theme in recent years concentrating on the experience and practice of prayer. I do not propose to repeat them, although there will inevitably be references to the life of prayer along the way. Rather, I shall examine the phenomenon of the deep in the Bible and make connections with a wide variety of human issues. There will be a degree of personal testimony too, from my own faith journey, from many personal contacts and from a recent visit to Estonia.

Today many people, schooled in the ways of the Enlightenment, look for answers to the most profound problems and expect faith to supply them. I cannot pretend that this is a book of clear 'answers' because many of the questions raised are part of the mystery of life itself. My hope and prayer is that this book will provide some clues to bring encouragement to some who are struggling with the apparent absence of God in places they might expect to find him, and others who are wrestling with the God they thought they knew.

Michael Howard

Chapter 1

Estonia: Faith after the Soviet Deluge

Ah, the thunder of many peoples,
 they thunder like the thundering of the sea!
Ah, the roar of nations,
 they roar like the roaring of mighty waters!
The nations roar like the roaring of many waters,
but God will rebuke them . . .

(Isaiah 17.12–13)

On the night of 27–28 September 1994, the 15,000-tonne Estline ferry *Estonia* was sailing *en route* from Tallinn to Stockholm in Sweden carrying 803 passengers, 186 crew members and a car-deck load of 1,000 tonnes. Rapidly worsening weather and heavy seas in the Gulf of Finland forced the captain to reduce speed to 14 knots. At 12.55 a.m., several witnesses reported hearing loud metallic banging near the bow of the ship. No one on board realized at the time that the bow visor locking devices had failed under the impact of the strong waves, wrenching it loose. Twenty minutes later, the pressure of water forced the visor to shear off completely from its hinges, pulling the vehicle ramp fully open, and releasing huge waves into the car deck running the length of the ship, making her list to starboard. At 1.20 a.m. the ferry's radio operator sent out the first Mayday call. By 1.25 a.m., a second call reported the ship was listing 20, then 30 degrees to starboard. Then there was a sudden awful silence. The ship finally sank in icy seas and 84 metres of water, north-north-west of the island of Hiumaa around 1.50 a.m., before most of the passengers and crew had time to man the lifeboats. Some 501 Swedes and 284 Estonians drowned. Just 137 of the 989 people on board survived.[1]

Nations on both sides of the Baltic Sea were united in shock and grief. It was Europe's worst peacetime maritime disaster. Today, in Tallinn, a striking white cross stands in the grounds of the Maritime Museum near the Sea Gate through the old city walls on the way to the harbour. Nearby, a stark black arched span of metal, broken in the middle, and a 3-metre long granite table recording the names of those who died are a moving reminder of the pain and the unanswered questions which remain for their grieving relatives, the ship designers and maritime safety agencies.

A nation that refused to be swept away

It was a miracle anyone survived the overwhelming of the ferry *Estonia* in a few short minutes, that terrible September night in 1994. Yet the story of these survivors is a kind of living parable of the history of the Estonian nation, again and again. This little country of 1.5 million people, tucked away in the north-east corner of the Baltic Sea, has had to come to terms with waves of a very different kind in the last thousand years. It has been successively invaded by armies of Vikings, Germans, Danes, Swedes, Poles and Russians so many times that it is a miracle Estonian identity has survived at all.

In June 1940, as Germany invaded France, Soviet forces occupied Estonia and *de facto* made it a republic of the Soviet Union. Shortly after, over 100,000 people, the cream of pre-war independent Estonian society including politicians, civil servants, teachers, engineers and clergy, were crammed into cattle trucks at bayonet point on their way to their enforced exile, where thousands died of cold, starvation and disease. Soon after, Hitler's forces occupied Estonia, until they were driven out by the Russians again in September 1944, when around 70,000 escaped to the West via Sweden, and another 30,000 were deported. After the war, the Soviet authorities deliberately encouraged Russians to come and settle in Estonia and a further 80,000 Estonians were deported in 1949. This huge movement of population reduced the ethnic population by 25 per cent in a few short terrible years, tearing the heart out of the nation's life.[2]

For the next 47 years, Estonia was under the cruel sea of harsh Soviet rule. Heavy industry was developed along the north coast, without any consideration of chemical, atmospheric and environmental pollution. Huge missile, submarine and air bases were built along the shoreline as Estonian shores became the first line of defence against any anticipated NATO nuclear attack. What remained of its ethnic population had to be subservient to the whims of its overlords in the Kremlin. But not for ever. Open protests against Soviet rule began in 1987, and independence was restored in August 1991. Despite such a troubled past, the remarkable, bloodless, Singing Revolution, which brought freedom and hope again, attracted worldwide admiration. No one can doubt the vitality of the new Estonia; a nation raised from the depths of near extinction.

Fifty years of Soviet religious oppression

Estonia has been a Christian country for eight centuries. In the census of 1934, over 78 per cent of the population claimed to be Lutheran, and 19 per cent Orthodox. The Soviet occupation and annexation was an unmitigated disaster for Christian believers. The churches were bereft of most of their clergy and many of their most able lay members. The Lutheran Church alone lost 162 pastors between 1939 and 1945 – almost 85 per cent of those in office in 1938. Most were murdered, deported to Siberia or banned from office. By the end of the war, only 92 out of 202 church buildings escaped damage or desecration by Soviet troops.[3] What then were the limits to public religious observance? Protestant clergy could preach, with censorship, but they were not allowed to teach children, or to engage in normal pastoral care, or any charitable activity.

Things were a little easier among believers within the Orthodox Church. Estonia was incorporated as a diocese of the Moscow patriarchate in 1945, no doubt in the hope that it would assist in promoting the Soviet grip on the population. This move alienated ethnic Estonian-speaking Orthodox believers. Nevertheless, Orthodoxy provided a real haven for faithful Christians right throughout this period.

Marxist propaganda was formidable. Every school and university subjected students to a barrage of atheistic propaganda from an early age. Virtually all religious literature was banned, and practically none was printed during the whole period. The Soviet authorities attempted to replace baptism with an atheistic 'child's name day', and countered confirmation with paid holidays for young people called 'summer youth days'. They had considerable success, backing up the institution of new civil ceremonies with rewards for participants, and with sanctions for those still opting for church baptisms, weddings and funerals. In the 1970s fewer than 10 per cent of the people were officially said to believe in a God, but this is almost certain to be low, because employment and university places were under constant threat.[4]

Mercifully, restrictions on believing began to ease several years before Mikhail Gorbachev abolished the old Stalinist Law on Religious Associations throughout the Soviet Union in 1990.[5] People came flooding back to the churches in the period 1989–91. Depleted numbers of clergy were ill-prepared to meet the sudden and overwhelming demand for baptism and confirmation. These numbers have not been maintained in the new atmosphere of freedom. Only time will tell whether this just represented passive worshippers claiming their religious rights in a more favourable political climate, or whether it was an early sign of long-term spiritual revival. Fifty years of Soviet rule have left terrible scars on Estonia, environmental as well as social and spiritual, which will take a long time to heal.

Courageous clergy

In August 1941, the theology faculty at Tartu University was closed, its members dismissed or imprisoned, and 70,000 volumes destroyed in the university library.[6] This deprived the Lutheran Church of new clergy at a stroke, but all was not lost. The present lively Theological Institute in Tallinn began in the late 1940s under the harmless enough title of Commission for Religious Affairs. The first principal was Elmar Salumaa, professor of systematic theology before the war, following his return from ten years in Siberia. With colleagues like Ewald Saag, an outstanding linguist, and Ago Viljari, who later directed the Institute into the mid-1980s, he arranged part-time correspondence courses, evening classes, and tutorials in their own homes or out in the countryside when necessary. Books and papers were either remembered or copied, sometimes ten typed sheets at once, on carbon paper. Since then, Toomas Paul, a pupil of Saag, has become a major academic theologian while never ceasing his pastoral duties. He has translated the New Testament into modern Estonian, and has been recognized internationally as a judicious and accurate chronicler of the modern history of the Estonian church. Such men became fathers-in-God to a new generation of Lutheran clergy. With great courage and wisdom they managed to keep academic and devotional study alive within the restrictions imposed by the Soviet authorities, and to be an inspiring example to their students.

Gustav Kutsar is one of the new breed of Lutheran clergy. He had no Christian upbringing, and came to Tallinn to study at the age of 15. He soon became aware of pro-communist bias in subjects like history and wondered how he could find the real truth. In 1982, he received a cross from a Czech girl in an exchange of gifts during a visit there as a student. His communist minder tore it off him in anger, but later he was able to save it secretly. From that moment on, he began to question what it might mean to bear the cross.

Kutsar then started to visit churches, and was befriended by an old man, while visiting an open church, who helped him to understand the meaning of the Christian symbols. In 1983, he finished studies at his trade school, and started a law study course, but withdrew after a time because the whole curriculum was oppressively dominated by the thought of Marx and Lenin. He had been a karate enthusiast until this was banned by the authorities, but continued his personal spiritual and physical development through yoga, fasting and meditation. A friend asked him once whether he was afraid to die. This question haunted him until in 1987 he went to the island of Saaremaa for a holiday with this same friend. They both decided they wanted to do something good for the Church. A young pastor at the nearby church at Kaarma set them to work restoring walls and floors, followed by similar work in the churches of Valjala and Karja. Discussions with him led at last to finding the answers to his questions about life and death, releasing him from fear. At the end of the summer, he and all his family were baptized.[7] He is now pastor of the Valjala congregation himself, and has planted a new church centre in Orissare, 20 miles away, where there has never been a worshipping congregation. He has a passion to bring spiritual renewal to the whole island.

A church which refused to die

The history of the Methodists in Estonia encapsulates much of a struggle to maintain Christian faith among the large denominations through war and occupation. In March 1944, the Central Methodist church in Tallinn was destroyed by Soviet bombs in the most devastating single air-raid suffered by the city. When members of the congregation gathered on the site of the blackened ruins next morning, their pastor Alexander Kuum noticed part of the font intact among the rubble, with the words 'Let the children come to me' written there. He remarked that he believed this to be a word from God for his fellow pastors and people to bring the love of Jesus Christ to a new generation. The second Methodist church in Tallinn at Kopli lasted until July 1950, when the building was seized by the Red Army for a radio station. After losing two church buildings, Tallinn Methodists were able to rent the Seventh Day Adventist congregational chapel, an unusual heaven-sent touch of ecumenical partnership, so that the building was full each Saturday and Sunday!

The present superintendent minister, Olav Pärnamets, remembers that morning when, as a boy of seven, his church was destroyed. Later, while attending an underground prayer meeting led by Kuum in 1951, he offered his life to God and determined to become a pastor. Training for ministry was only possible through an underground network of theological seminars with few Bibles, or other books. A fearless evangelist, Kuum was considered so dangerous that he was deported to Siberia in 1952, but in an amnesty granted by Khrushchev was unexpectedly released in 1956, when he continued to lead Estonian Methodists for a further 10 years.

Kuum's successor in Tallinn during the Stalinist period was Hugo Oengo. Oengo was a lecturer in civil engineering at the City Technical University as well as being an outstanding lay preacher.[8] The Soviet authorities put him under intense pressure to renounce his faith, because of his position in the university. When they had no success, they insisted he had to do one job or the other. Oengo chose to become a pastor, and left his university post without compensation. After he left his university post, the authorities forced him to hand his savings over in exchange for 'investment certificates'. Each year, a draw would be made and money prizes given to lucky 'investors'. The following year, Oengo won first prize, and a fair amount of his money back. This happened twice more, and he won two more prizes. The KGB were so embarrassed, they abandoned the scheme in Estonia, and severely disciplined the officials who ran it! Soon after, the Soviet authorities were desperately trying to complete a new underground submarine base at Paldiski down the coast, but were frustrated by flooding caused by hidden silt channels in the dolomite caverns. In desperation, under pressure from a tight Defence Ministry deadline, they consulted Oengo. He agreed to supervise the completion of the project, provided the KGB ceased persecuting Christian leaders of all denominations, gave him his pastorate income back, and reduced restrictions on Christian meetings! Oengo's resolution stimulated an increase of 700 in the church congregation between 1953 and 1962 through 'revival preaching weeks', and clandestine home Bible study and prayer groups.

When independence was regained, the city of Tallinn offered the Methodists a magnificent site for a new church near the harbour, opposite the entrance to Kadriorg Park. Prizewinning Estonian architects produced a radical 'Noah's Ark' design for this new Mission Centre, to be a theological college as well as a 700-seat church to train pastors throughout the Baltic area. Finance for the project has come from South Korea and the USA. This building, topped by a tower in the form of a sail with a large cross, is an inspiring contemporary statement of Christian faith for the new millennium.

Springs of faith

During my recent visit to Estonia, one pastor mentioned three factors that helped to sustain faith through the Soviet period as 'the grace of God, and the prayers of old clergy, and of old women'! That grace of God was clearly displayed among this remarkable people in six notable ways.

1 *In the music they played and sang*

It is difficult to imagine the elation felt by the 300,000-strong crowd of singers in national costume who participated in the annual national song festival which preceded the return to independence! It is estimated that in the late 1980s one in twenty in the population was a regular member of a choir. Some churches had up to six choirs for different ages and functions! The communists could censor sermons, but they couldn't censor oratorios, hymns or songs, although they recognized their power to move people's hearts. In some areas, restrictions were placed on performances of music by J. S. Bach as well as Estonian composers like Rudolf Tobias (1873–1918) and Artur Kapp (1878–1952) who wrote motets and chorale preludes on biblical themes, because it was believed that they would inflame national feeling.

Choral music did far more than that. It was a primary means of evangelism. Choral music taught the gospel to children and young people when they were not allowed to meet for Christian instruction. Such music provided a way for Christians to affirm their beliefs when they were not allowed to profess their faith openly in any other way. Choral music provided a means of informal Christian fellowship. Young people joined a choir, sometimes even when they knew they could not really sing, to meet like-minded friends, and be bathed in word and song with an integrity not found in any communist youth organization! Choral music gave them all hope and access to God as their spirits were stirred deep within – in the very place where he was able to speak to them.

But it was not just the singing that affirmed Christian belief, and drew the uncommitted to worship Christ for themselves. The music had a spirit in itself which became the vehicle of the Holy Spirit. People of no particular Christian background who are now organists, teachers and civil servants testified to me of the spirit of the music which pointed them to God during their teenage years, and led them over a period of several years to confirmation, and regular church membership. Music for them had a touch of sacramental mystery about it which is not always recognized by worshippers with a well-defined Protestant theology. This is also true of other subjects which people went on to study at depth at university. An Estonian Ministry of Defence planner spoke to me of his undergraduate mathematics studies at Tartu university, something that couldn't be warped by Marxist spin, giving him a framework to think freely about philosophy and God. Others found faith in their own words through the spirits of poetry and graphic art, which allowed them to express their humanity freely.

Fifty years of spiritual deprivation of the normal channels of Christian sustenance through word and sacrament seem to have heightened Estonians' awareness of contemporary art, music, literature and poetry as vehicles for spirituality. Concerts of avant-garde orchestral music, including some by living Estonian composers, are packed out at the beautifully restored National Concert Hall. Arvo Pärt (b. 1935), exiled for much of his adult life, is celebrated as one of the world's leading choral composers. Pärt's music, with its minimalist concentration on particular notes and harmonies, provides space for contemplation. It is spare, 'pure' music of remarkable beauty. In recent years Pärt has concentrated on biblical themes.

The lifting of the Iron Curtain has revealed some other gifted composers with a growing international reputation. They include Veljo Tormis (b. 1930), whose search for the musical identity of his nation has led him to write stirring choral music celebrating the links between human life and work and the yearly cycle of nature using the rhythms of ancient Nordic runic poetry. His *Curse upon Iron* (1972) is a remarkable choral protest against the life-destructive forces of evil from the middle of the Soviet period.

Shelter us now, supreme Creator!
Keep us safe, God Almighty!
So that mankind should not perish . . .
. . . New eras, New gods,
and cannons and aeroplanes
and tanks and machine guns.
New iron and steel.
Brand-new, intelligent
precise powerful killers . . .
. . . Paralyze and knock out of action,
obliterate, disable,
wound, list missing,
and kill, kill with iron and steel . . .
. . . Ohoy villain! Evil iron!
Blade of the sword, mother of war![9]

This poem was adapted from the Finnish national epic *Kalevala* and supplemented by Estonian poets Paul-Eerik Rummo and Jaan Kaplinski. It is not hard to see why such an explosive text spoke to the hearts of the Estonian people when it was first performed.

Urmas Sisask (b. 1960) composes in a more meditative style. His moving *Estonian Mass* was performed by a choir of 30,000 at the National Song Festival in 1993. Sisask 'considers the mass to be a great mystery helping human beings to communicate with the higher invisible reality. The *Estonian Mass* is part of the culture of the Estonians, the culture which keeps the nation alive.'[10] Not exactly orthodox Christian theology, but a profound response to the greater power of the Spirit of God over hostile ideology.

2 *In the churches they kept open*

The little band of clergy who remained after Stalin's purges were but a fraction of their pre-war numbers. The Soviet authorities judged them not dangerous enough to deport with the rest. Yet they proved to be heroes of faith, whose story will probably never be fully told. They ministered without proper support for as long as age and health allowed. Where no clergy were available, choir leaders, sunday-school teachers and lay preachers did what they could to maintain worship, prayer and a Christian presence. People walked many miles just to enter a church building even once a month. Other more casual visitors could wander in out of curiosity where churches remained open. There they could see the evocative architecture, the holy symbols of faith, and meet old men and women to explain what it all meant; listen to the organ play music with biblical titles, and let the Holy Spirit do his work.

There is controversy even today among some of the survivors about the extent of collaboration alleged in order that the church could continue to function, and the clergy continue to do their work of pastoral care. One wise pastor remarked to me, 'The greatest need today among older clergy, is forgiveness.' This is just one symptom of the inevitable fall-out from such a period of intense suffering and dislocation of normal human relationships.

What is clear is that the church in Estonia was God's Church, and that even at the moment when the authorities were writing it off as a spent force, people were hearing the call to ordination. Lorna and Michael Bourdeaux have written eloquently about Harri Mötsnik, who committed the unforgiveable sin in 1970 of giving up a legal career at the age of 42 to become a Lutheran pastor and fearless preacher. He was mercilessly harassed by the KGB until his health gave way in 1985. In his passionate denunciation of the Soviet restrictions, he proved equally embarrassing to his ecclesiastical superiors, who feared that their carefully crafted *modus vivendi* with the civil authorities might be threatened.[11] Other young men followed, some after national service in the Soviet army, or university training. The seed for some was sown while doing voluntary repair work on church buildings which had fallen into disrepair. They expressed their commitment to the faith by restoring the roofs, floors and paintwork! One electrical engineer I met began his ordination evening classes at the Theological Institute while maintaining the boilers at the Tallinn Botanical Gardens.

3 Through the sustenance of Christian family life

Most, though not all, of the present clergy who heard the call to ordination in the 1970s and 1980s came from strong Christian families. Some followed their fathers' footsteps into the ministry. The importance of the family and of family memories in Soviet times cannot be overestimated, in enabling God to speak in an atmosphere of militant atheism. With such huge displacements of population after the war, there were few Estonian families that did not have one member at least in Siberia. In such circumstances, there were two main ways to be close to them, and to keep their memory alive among the next generation. One was prayer, and the other was to keep hanging on to what they stood for, and were suffering for. Both led to Christian faith and to the Church. The most dislocated family was still the one place which provided an alternative to the standards of truth and lifestyle being advocated at school, at university and in the workplace. Nevertheless, informers were so numerous and the KGB so devious, that there was always a danger that the securest of families could be infiltrated and subtly pressurized to conform. People used to say 'a good Russian joke could only be repeated three times; once among good friends, then to the person next to you on the train to Siberia, lastly among your fellow inmates in the labour camps'.

Families were still the safest place to explore believing as children grew up. Without Sunday schools, it was in the home that children could learn Bible stories and receive answers to their questions with integrity. Christian teaching was publicly and regularly ridiculed by teachers in schools, before children from the ages of six or seven. But no teacher could ever get as close to a child at that age as a Christian parent, and children remember. During my visit, clergy and lay people spoke time and again of the example of parents and grandparents, and of the quality of their lifestyle, which led them to believe.

It is here that grandparents, and particularly grandmothers, feature so much in the memory of Estonian Christians. It is humbling to think of old women as major evangelists of the nation! Parents were out at work for long hours. Grandparents were there for the children when they came home from school. 'I remember my grandmother laying hands on me, and praying for me at the age of five. She died shortly after. I can still feel her hands on me.' 'My grandmother asked me as a young girl to read Bible stories to her because cataracts impaired her sight. Although I didn't find a faith until I walked into a church many years later, I never forgot those Bible stories, which laid the foundation for believing.' 'I remember my grandmother teaching me a prayer when I was a young child of three and a half. While facing a difficult decision serving in the Soviet Army in the Ukraine, the prayer came back to me, word for word. It was the first step on my path to ordination.' Such inspiring remarks are typical among adult believers in Estonia today.

4 *Speaking through the natural environment*

For such a small country, visitors cannot help being moved by the impression of immense space. There are few hills to break the seemingly endless vista of lakes and forests. This, with the subtle effects of the Baltic light, makes for an air of beauty and mystery. My visit coincided with particularly good September weather, after an appallingly wet summer. I saw how the hidden sun can turn autumn mists into a strange blue haze like a deep sea, from which individual trees emerge like ghosts as one moves towards them, and copses like sleepy sea-monsters.

Sunsets too in Estonia are magical, with the dark shapes of trees etched out against the clear golden glow of the western sky. Add a lake or the seashore to the picture, and the effect is of a vast natural cathedral which is infused with the glory of God and which raises questions about life and the limitations of materialism. Here is what Mircea Eliade would call a *hierophany*, the manifestation of the sacred in things part and parcel of the natural world.[12] These sights come season after season, year after year, and appear in sharp contrast to the drab, Soviet-inspired architecture that disfigures nearly every urban community. Something of this natural implicit spirituality of the land is captured by Jaan Kaplinski:

> The worlds of people and of trees are so different. But still,
> there is something so human, almost intelligible,
> in that tangle of branches. It is like a script,
> like a language that I do not understand, although I know
> that what is written there
> has long been known to me; it cannot be much different
> from what can be read in books,
> hands, or face.[13]

Urbanization is a recent gloss on Estonian life. At their heart, Estonians are a rural people with a love of nature, and of the land. They understand this kind of language. Even urban Estonians bury their dead in forest cemeteries. They like their loved ones to have their own tree next to their grave as a symbol of new life and hope, and churches reinforce this faith with open-air cemetery services at seasons like All Saints. The Soviet authorities recognized the power of these services, and made special efforts to combat them in their own rival secular funeral rites.

5 *In prominent representations of the cross of Christ*

The vast spaces of the skylines of Estonia are punctuated by large crosses on top of church spires. In Tallinn, despite the height of the Olympia and Viru hotels, the huge spires of the old northern-Gothic style churches dominate, together with that of the new Methodist church. Although the Soviet authorities used the spire of the Oleviste church for a KGB communications array, they never removed the cross on top. Many older churches are often half as high again as the all-pervading woodland, their roofs and their crosses standing out above the trees in rural areas. In older times, tracks and roads from village to village led to the churches, and so implicitly to the cross. Much of this pattern still remains and gives an impression to visitors that whatever happens in the nation's history, it is under the protection of the cross of Christ. There is no doubt the communists recognized the power of the cross as a symbol to move people's hearts. They removed crosses where they could and even refused to allow the cross to appear on memorials in cemeteries for much of the Soviet period.

A particular instance illustrates this near the shoreline in the city's beautiful Kadriorg Park. A century before the *Estonia* disaster, the Russian warship *Russalka* sank in a storm outside Tallinn harbour, with the loss of 177 sailors. They are remembered by a statue of a mighty bronze angel holding a golden cross in her right hand stretched out over the sea. The *Russalka* angel is a popular attraction for sightseers. In Soviet times, many couples had their wedding photographs taken under the cross after the official state ceremony as a way of receiving God's blessing on their future life together. Whether faith or mere superstition, the authorities took a dim view of this, enough to threaten any contemplating such action who were in ideologically sensitive occupations.

6 *Through the prayers and support of the world Church*

It is sometimes said that history belongs to the intercessors, and I believe this to be true. Throughout the long dark night of twentieth-century communist power, untold numbers of prayers were being made for subject peoples like the people of Estonia, and their masters as well. Like the Jerusalem Christians praying for St Peter in prison, few of us believed our prayers could be so dramatically answered as in the breach of the Berlin Wall, and the sudden dismantling of the Soviet military apparatus in Eastern Europe, when it happened. Support was also there in a more tangible way. For many years, Finns were allowed to visit Tallinn on the ferry, provided they did not stray beyond the city limits. It provided the regime with useful foreign currency, but also aided the supply of desperately needed Bibles and other Christian literature. Estonians speak highly of radio broadcasting like the BBC World Service. This provided a lifeline for those who could receive it, and an immaculate standard of reporting to measure reality against propaganda.

Wave upon wave of persecution meant that the soul of Estonia experienced an enforced 'dark night' during the whole of this period. But God was there, explicitly or implicitly in the depths of the culture and psyche of Estonia and her people. Furthermore, the way the Soviet authorities went about indoctrinating the people in atheist dogma was counterproductive. To Estonians with their history of faith it seemed too much like special pleading. The constant hammering from every organ of the party apparatus, that there was no God, forced many Estonians to consider there might be an alternative. It made spirituality an exciting quest for nonconformists!

Today, the communist legacy is there for all to experience in widespread unbelief and cynicism. But for some Estonians, the experience of confronting dark and evil forces that threatened to overwhelm them has actually contributed to the experience and growth of faith. It remains to be seen whether a people whose culture and faith proved so resilient under the waves of Soviet persecution can survive the swift advance of a much more attractive prospect: unprincipled Western consumerism.

Chapter 2

The Power of the Sea

Let us think of the sea. And that there is something greater than all questions.
Something that reaches over all borders.
Water, foam, stones, sand.
Wind.
Sometimes warm, sometimes cold.[1]

In the last chapter we portrayed the recent history of Estonia using the imagery of the sea. The hostile power of the Soviet state acted like a veritable flood, attempting to drown the spirits of the people by wave upon wave of propaganda, and sink the nation in the deep with it. The story of the years since independence was restored shows just how superficial that atheistic veneer was, once the constraints of an oppressive state apparatus were taken away. A nation plunged into the depths for fifty years is surfacing again, and being recreated with new vigour and enterprise as it enjoys the freedom to rediscover itself. The scars of this awful baptism will mark the people and the landscape for many years to come, but there is an infectious spirit of hope especially among the younger people once more.

The awesome motifs of water and sea are particularly apt to describe the scary hidden forces unleashed by the exercise of political and military power and the upheaval it brings to human lives. In this chapter we shall explore more of this mysterious nature of water, the sea and the deep, and the way it can represent spiritual and psychological forces affecting us as individuals and nations, or indeed the future of civilization itself.

Water is hydrogen and oxygen, two of the basic building-blocks of life. Human beings are over 70 per cent water, and cannot survive for more than a few days without it. Yet water is strangely ambivalent in human experience. We all know it in its common forms as liquid, solid and vapour. Each of these can bring refreshment and delight to us, or inflict pain, discomfort, terrible suffering and death upon us. Again, pure water is completely transparent, but a deep pool of pure water is dark and mysterious. Light is reflected in water, lending it a remarkable variety of visual effects. Light is also refracted by water, so that it distorts the images of the objects it contains when seen from above the surface. Water is the staff of life, yet deadly. Transparent, yet dark. Honest and down to earth yet deeply mysterious and fickle. Water lends itself to picture language in myriad different ways. No wonder it is one of the chief pigments in the artist's palette of painters, authors and composers. When water becomes the sea, all these properties and effects are magnified so that the sea, with its salty tang, takes on a distinctive personality or spirituality all its own. The sea then becomes a multi-faceted symbol for life and death, beauty and power, mood and hidden depths and inner turbulence, in nature, people, human society, history and politics. In the Bible, the sea represents all these, and an extra dimension as well. In the ceaseless chaotic movements of the sea we can detect the creative and redemptive power of the living God at work on the raw material which makes up the very genesis of the cosmos.

This theological symbolism, which we shall be exploring during the rest of the book, is well expressed by the constant refrain of Arthur Ainger's famous hymn

> God is working his purpose out as year succeeds to year;
> God is working his purpose out and the time is drawing near –
> Nearer and nearer draws the time, the time that shall surely be,
> When the earth shall be filled with the glory of God, as the waters cover the sea.

This refrain is a conflation of two verses from the classic period of Old Testament prophecy in Isaiah 11 and Habakkuk 2. They portray the hope of a world one day when 'the earth shall be filled with the knowledge of the glory of the Lord'. Some translations speak of this 'filling' as like the water filling the sea. But in the Bible, the emphasis is more on the way the water is a 'cover' or visible and poetic representation of the mysterious personality of the sea. It is more a 'God's eye view', like the earth seen from space. We must now try to unpack this poetic symbolism.

Creation and re-creation

In his studies of the origin of religions, Mircea Eliade describes water as symbolizing 'the primal substance from which all forms come, and to which they will return, either by their own regression, or in a cataclysm. Because it incorporates in itself all potential, water becomes a symbol of life ("living water"). Rich in seeds, it fertilizes earth, animals, and women. It contains in itself all possibilities, it is supremely fluid, it sustains the development of all things.'[2] So water and the sea represent the very stuff out of which creation is born and develops. This primal, generative quality of water reaching back to the origin of time is described by Jaan Kaplinski:

> The sea, of which so little now remains.
> Sometimes it is memory, sometimes our own blood . . .
> Sometimes sea water, which in Norway during the war was used
> for blood transfusions, when there was not enough blood.
> Sometimes it is a warm salty source in woman's, your body, in
> which once again the miracle of union recurs.
> You sense something, like a thread, a cord along which
> Cambrian, Jurassic, Tertiary, earlier centuries send their
> messages to future times which do not yet have names,
> to countries, kingdoms which do not yet have names.
> To peoples who speak languages which do not yet have names,
> You are on your way there, sperm, chromosomes, tiny egoistical
>   genes.
> I believe that you are a message – then I am the commentary
> of that message, its translation into flesh and blood . . .[3]

Water is one of the four primal elements of ancient wisdom, along with earth, air and fire. From the beginning, whether in worldwide mythology, the Bible, or in science, water is the cradle of all things and all life. In the Babylonian 'Genesis' myth, for example, Apsu, the primeval sweet-water ocean, Tiamat, his consort, the salt-water ocean, and their son Mummu, the mist rising between the two, contained all the elements out of which the universe was formed. The Bible begins with God and the awesome 'deep'. More than this, from earliest times immersion in water symbolizes a return to the chaotic formless state so that the self can be 'reconstituted'. Emergence from the water then is in effect a regeneration, a reforming or reordering of being; a repetition of the act of creation. Water thus is 'living', purifying, restorative and healing. It is easy to see how the mythology of many cultures extended its power to become the agent of eternal life. Christian baptism has many antecedents. Of course, this life might not be accessible to everyone. In ancient mythology it is guarded by a variety of monsters, or else it is difficult or dangerous to get to. It is only available to those who pass the tests of skill, initiative and endurance.

This psychological variation on the theme, the notion of the sea-journey as a trial or proof of human worth, is found not only in myth, like the Greek Odyssey, but in actual sea journeys, where water represents the distance between what a person is and what they could become. Typical of the genre, and a personal favourite, is the story of *Rinaldo*, because of its musical setting as a dramatic cantata by Brahms. Goethe's poem, set in the story of the crusades, describes a valiant knight who has been enticed away from his battle to liberate Jerusalem by the beautiful Armida, who lives on an enchanted island. His fellow knights come to find him, and urge him to return to the battle.

To the shore, to the ship!
Though the wind be not favourable to you yet,
ardently grasp the oars!
Here let the strong man prove himself;
thus we shall race through the waves![4]

The decisive moment in the story comes when Rinaldo sees himself in a mystic diamond shield, and realizes what depths his infatuation has brought him to. He is shaken, and resolves to return to the fray. Armida's beauty and the magical landscape then fade as he joins his friends on the journey back across the sea to renew the struggle for the Holy Land. In Brahms's setting, the most exciting music comes as the dolphins join in the general delight as the friends, now united in purpose, sail back towards the path of duty.

The sea's personality

Water is personified in Greek mythology. Living babbling water describes the life of playful, seductive nymphs, minor feminine divinities, not always as innocuous as at first sight, providing an ambivalent human reaction of fear and fascination. The angry sea, by contrast, takes on a fiercely masculine aspect. Jean Sibelius portrays both, especially the playful personalities of the sea sprites, in his magnificent orchestral tone poem *The Oceanides*, as does Antonin Dvořák in his touching opera *Rusalka*. To the Greeks, Poseidon was the god of the ocean, and his symbol was the trident, which originally represented the teeth of the sea monsters. He was also god of earthquakes, which the Greeks thought were caused by the shock waves of a wild sea battering the cliffs of the coastline, not in fact so very far from current geological understanding! This symbolism is extended to the flood mythology, widespread in many ancient cultures. It is here that we encounter the idea of re-creation on a cosmic scale. Most of the mythic traditions contain the idea of the universe being subject to periodic deluges where one era is overwhelmed, submerged, reconstituted into its component elements and reborn to be inhabited by new people. The biblical stories of the Creation and the Flood and their ancient Mesopotamian analogues belong to this same family of images.

Ancient mythology points up many of the ambivalent feelings people still have about the sea or the deep. These have provided inspiration for some of the finest authors and painters and the greatest music. No one has captured the moods of the sea better than Claude Debussy in his symphonic sketches, *La Mer*. Debussy was the son of a sailor. He was constantly enthralled by the stories his father told him of the journeys he had made to distant parts of the world. As he grew up he toyed with the idea of following his father's footsteps in time-honoured manner, going away to sea to prove himself, before realizing his temperamental limitations. A frequent visitor to art galleries in London and Paris, he was deeply moved by the sea paintings of Turner, and the landscapes and seascapes of two popular Japanese artists of the day, Katsushika Hokusai and Ando Hiroshige. The composer requested a reproduction of a Hokusai print to be the cover design on the full orchestral score. In this beautiful music, melody, harmony and rhythm are combined to represent a fusion of nature and art, often reflecting the oriental nature of the paintings that inspired it.

Joseph Conrad, himself a sailor in his younger days, and one of the most perceptive of all the writers of sea stories, takes this theme one stage further. To him, the mariner who has to come to terms with the ways of the deep is a true artist in his own right.

> Like all true art, the general conduct of a ship and her handling in particular cases had a technique which could be discussed with delight and pleasure by men who found in their work, not bread

alone, but an outlet for the peculiarities of their temperament. To get the best and truest effect from the infinitely varying moods of sky and sea, not pictorially, but in the spirit of their calling, was their vocation, one and all; and they recognized this with as much sincerity, and drew as much inspiration from this reality as any man who has ever put brush to canvas.[5]

The deep, and the risk of faith

The sea, then, can be a delight. Holidays by the sea are eagerly looked forward to for refreshment and renewal of body, mind and spirit. Honeymoons by the sea seem to represent all the possibilities for two people reaching out into the unknown in their partnership. The deep represents challenge, adventure, and unknown possibilities to be discovered, developed and enjoyed.

Sometimes when you
Look at the sky
Synged pink
by evening's
breath
Or take a walk
by the Sea
Barefoot through
Seaweed tangled
Waves in Sensual
tease
advancing
Subsiding
The ocean's Wet
frothing mouth
Licking your
feet
gasping
the drowning
Light
Watching it Fade
The moon rising
The blueness of night
filling your eyes

your head by
Sea salt
intoxicated
A mystic moment –
Felt once.
Remembered for
Eternity.[6]

Yet there is risk, peril and the possibility of failure and heartbreak for every pair of lovers moved by romantic seaside settings. The sea represents the adventure of faith through life as they 'launch out into the deep' with confidence together without knowing the future, but believing that their destiny is somehow contained by the vision of the water. But the water which represents their dreams of the future together can also be capricious and uncertain, giving them 'the blues'. They set out in faith not knowing whether that which unites their thoughts and feelings in the beginning will divide them by the end of their life's journey, because of sea-changes in their circumstances.

Dark and fearsome mystery

The sea is the deepest, darkest part of the surface of the natural world. The ocean floor remains one of the last unexplored areas on earth, and is likely to remain so for a very long time. Less than 5 per cent of the topography of the deep is mapped in detail. The Marianas Trench in the Pacific is 10,924 metres below sea level, more than 2,000 metres more than Mount Everest is high. These depths consist of vast mountain ranges, deep canyons, mighty steaming lava flows. The sea floor is on the move at an incredible 18 centimetres a year in the eastern Pacific. For just below the crust at the bottom of the oceans is another even deeper and more mysterious layer, the molten magma of volcanic eruptions, ceaselessly active in subcrustal currents which are still separating continents, building mountains, and affecting climatic patterns. In the creation of new volcanic islands we can see for ourselves the power of these forces reworking the topography of the deep ocean floor. In great earthquakes, we can feel the movement of the twenty or more giant plates that make up the earth's crust around the earth's circumference.

Life began in the deep, and is sustained by the deep, and new life is still being discovered in deep-sea exploration; weird creatures in a pitch-black environment, enduring fantastic pressures. Other oceanic creatures roaming nearer the surface are equally mysterious. We know very little about the community life of giant whales, and even less about the giant squid, which has become a legend in sailors' folklore. These monsters have a mythology all their own. They allow us to externalize what we hold in our own subconscious depths. These human projections have spawned a genus of legendary sea-creatures, like the elusive creature which is supposed to live in the depths of Loch Ness, *Jaws* of Hollywood fame, or the beastly creation featured in John Wyndham's 1950s sci-fi thriller, *The Kraken Wakes*. Films like *The Crimson Tide* and *The Hunt for Red October* have focused on those even more deadly and all too real monsters, giant nuclear-powered missile submarines, bigger than World War One battleships and with a million times more destructive potential. These terrifying weapons are the true incarnations of the ancient mythic gods of the deep, roaming the depths for months on end without surfacing. The deep is indeed a fascinating and fearful place and provides us with dark mysteries, in an age when mysteries are supposed to have been explained away.

No wonder this mysterious deep is to be feared. Innocent and playful one minute, it can be a raging life-threatening monster the next. Quite simply, the health of the deep is bound up with the future of civilization here on earth. The retreating ozone layer in the atmosphere, and the near-certainty of global warming with its attendant severe hurricanes, is causing serious concern as we enter a new millennium. A rise of a few metres in sea level following substantial melting of the Arctic and Antarctic icecaps, as predicted in the next hundred years, will wipe island paradises like the Maldives and Vanuatu from the map. It represents a huge potential threat to the lives, homes, crops, population centres and future of millions living at sea level, from the Ganges to the Nile deltas, and from the beachy vacationlands of Florida to the dykes and polders of the Netherlands.

Global warming will also exacerbate the *El Niño* effect, where profound changes in the temperature patterns of deep water in the western Pacific have been responsible for huge changes in sea and weather patterns in tropical and sub-tropical lands around the globe, in an eleven-year cycle affecting agriculture, fisheries and climatic models. Meanwhile on land, it is likely that the deep will shortly feature in a different way in future cross-border conflict. Some areas of the Middle East, while awash with oil, are potentially short of groundwater. As populations grow, pressure will grow on water resources both from rivers and from artesian wells. Unless water is conserved by international agreement soon, the volatile regimes of this desperately unstable region will have one more reason to start further wars. The deep represents many aspects of danger for the future of humanity, on land as well as sea.

A symbol of evil

Amid all its many moods and forms, it is easy to see why the sea and the deep form the most potent imaginable psychological symbol of evil and dread – a universal symbol affecting all periods of history, many cultures, and many faiths. Fascinating, capricious and deadly, some writers have hinted that it has all the features of the devil himself. Joseph Conrad explores this theme in the *Heart of Darkness*. His hero, Captain Marlow, recounts his experiences when as a young man setting off on the adventure of life he is poring over a map of the world, alighting on equatorial Africa. 'It had ceased to be a blank space of delightful mystery – a white patch for a boy to dream gloriously over. It had become a place of darkness. But there was in it one river especially, a mighty big river, that you could see on the map, resembling an immense snake uncoiled, with its head in the sea, its body at rest, curving afar over a vast country, and its tail lost in the depths of the land . . . Then I remembered there was a big concern, a Company for trade on that river. Dash it all! I thought to myself, they can't trade without using some kind of craft on that lot of fresh water – steamboats! Why shouldn't I try to get charge of one? I went on along Fleet Street, but could not shake off the idea. The snake had charmed me.'[7] The story describes his long sea and river journey into the heart of the Congo, where the character of a charismatic ivory trader first attracts and later repels him, forcing him to face up to the darkness in his own soul. It illustrates brilliantly so many aspects of the character of the sea – attraction, sinister mystery, and dark unpredictability. A lifetime's challenge and a risk to life itself. To survive an encounter with evil like this with integrity means nothing less than a revelation of inner moral and spiritual truth leading to greater personal maturity.

Death in the Baltic

Of course Conrad's Captain Marlow did not have to risk his life or his honour exploring the meaning of that snake on a map in the heart of Africa. Many others do not have the choice. 'Impenetrable and heartless, the sea has given nothing of itself to the suitors for its precarious favours. Unlike the earth, it cannot be subjugated at any cost of patience and toil . . . the most amazing wonder of the deep is its unfathomable cruelty.'[8] When tragedy strikes, particularly in loss of life involving an encounter with the deep, it raises huge questions about the existence of a good God for people of faith. When the ferry *Estonia* sank in the Gulf of Finland, the great majority of victims, 501 in all, were Swedish, sailing back home overnight after visiting Tallinn. The shock of the tragedy affected Sweden in a profound but very different way from Estonia. In Estonia, the sinking occurred just three years after independence. The memory of fifty painful years of personal and national dislocation of normal human relationships was all too real. They did not know anything else. The temperamentally reserved Estonians had learnt how to take tragedy in their stride. That does not mean they felt it less deeply. It just means that for many, one more disaster just continued the pattern inflicted on them through their recent history. They seemed to be more successful in coming to terms with their sorrow as a result, because they had had plenty of practice.

By contrast, Sweden has managed in the twentieth century to remain a neutral observer while most other European nations have been at war. The Swedish people have enjoyed a relatively untroubled growth of a high standard of living, with excellent state-provided social care. Everything has been done to minimize pain, and to provide each member of the population with a full and fulfilled life in an open and safe society. In such a situation the Church has been part of the service-and-consumer culture, providing suitable worship and ritual as required for private, seasonal and civic occasions. Sweden is reckoned to be one of the most secularized countries in Europe. Yet most people do have an implicit relationship with church, although this is strictly privatized, and for all but a small minority only becomes activated at the significant stages of life and death.

When the power of the deep shook Swedish society in the *Estonia* sinking, it was as though an atomic bomb had been dropped on it. In Sweden, the 'ferry situation' is well known, and corresponds to the 'football situation' in England. Most people knew it from the inside, and could imagine how it felt to escape from the narrow gangways among passengers in a state of panic. Few communities escaped bereavement. The shock-waves from the disaster are still being felt in a whole host of unanswered questions and accusations. The death that the deep dealt to hundreds of victims that awful night has had terrible lasting power.

Per Pettersson[9] has carefully chronicled reactions to the sinking in Sweden, and lessons to be learnt by the wider Church. He recalls how the press, and local and national radio and TV, were completely taken over by the disaster for the best part of a week. Twelve hours after the sinking, the Archbishop of Sweden was interviewed on the main lunchtime news. On the first evening, at least 500 churches around the country were kept open for individual prayer and the lighting of candles. Churches were safe places to meet to express grief, and huge numbers gathered to light candles. Bells were symbolically tolled. Congregations were unfamiliarly full of young faces and the media legitimized their being in church in the way they reported their sorrow and grief. Some lived through their own earlier griefs all over again. Committed Christians among the mourners and the survivors had opportunities to share what their faith means. It helped everyone to see King Karl Gustav and Queen Silvia with Prime Minister Carl Bildt weeping openly, sharing the national mood.

The clergy became existential interpreters of the situation through the questions of journalists. By common consent they really helped, articulating the thoughts and prayers of ordinary people. Bishop Martin Lonnebo remarked at the time: 'Many people's faith in God sank to the bottom with *M/S Estonia*. God is also at 86 metres depth in *Estonia*. God is the great mystery of life. He is life, he is death. God is with us although it is incomprehensible.'[10] Some people were greatly heartened by his words and felt able to agree with him. Many others were not so sure. But there was one positive outcome.

Pettersson points to the way encounter with the deep in the *Estonia* disaster made those not directly affected re-evaluate their attitude to life. Everyone was suddenly reminded of the fragility of life. One journalist wrote 'It exposes in a painful way the arrogance of our faith in technology.'[11] And another, 'Think about it, what is it that you really believe in? In Christian resurrection? In reincarnation? One can never protect oneself against the pain when someone dies. But a faith, a well reflected conviction is an enormous help.'[12]

The parable of the Titanic

In England no ocean sinking has hit the headlines like that of the White Star liner *Titanic*, the most famous wreck in history. *Titanic* went down off Newfoundland after hitting an iceberg in April 1912. *Titanic* was the largest liner in the world at the time, 46,329 tons and 882 feet long, with an intricate set of hull compartments which her designers confidently predicted would make her unsinkable. She was sailing on a prestige run from Southampton to New York, and sank in 2 hours 40 minutes on a clear night in a calm sea off Newfoundland with the loss of 1,523 lives. Endless books have been written to try to answer the question of blame – the builders who provided too few lifeboats, the captain who should have taken the threat of icebergs more seriously, the radio operator who omitted to pass on a crucial message, the crew who should have rehearsed boat drill the day before, among others. But a huge ship steaming at 22 knots through an iceberg zone at night would always be in danger without proper navigational radar. It is a miracle more liners on the North Atlantic run at that time did not founder the same way.

Now consider the year, 1912. It was the peak of British self-confidence in the world, yet just two years from a world war which was to bring an irrevocable alteration in the balance of power to Western civilization and the certainties it embodied. In this catastrophe we have a dramatic parable and prophecy of the passing of an age. Why then has the *Titanic* story such an appeal now, three generations later? Because it has taken the best part of a century and two world wars for the truths it symbolizes to grip public imagination.

James Cameron's *Titanic* is the most successful film ever. It cost $200 million to make, and netted global takings of $1.8 billion even before the video was released. *Titanic* is not just the recreation of a tragedy that happened before most of us were born. It is a Millennial film, in which the doomed passengers sailing to a new world have a sense of destiny about them. The North Atlantic represents the gap between their present lives and the glorious future that beckons them in America. The *Titanic* held a complete cross-section of human society in its first-, second- and third-class accommodation. Hence its enormous appeal to a wide variety of audiences at the end of the old millennium! The way Hollywood weaves the tragic love story played by Kate Winslet and Leonardo di Caprio into the plot adds an extra dimension to the symbolism and grips the audience. In the story of *Titanic*, the cruel deep in the form of the iceberg stops the unstoppable progress of an age that thought it could create its own glorious future on the back of its own technological genius, and fatally holes it. In the very year 'the unsinkable' *Titanic* went down, Sir Edward Elgar was setting the bombastic words of Arthur O'Shaughnessy in his choral epic *The Music Makers*.

> With wonderful deathless ditties we build the world's great cities
> And out of a fabulous story we fashion an empire's glory . . .

Titanic with her seven passenger decks slowly going down into the water with all lights blazing and the band playing gives the lie to all that. The drowning of an empire stratified rigidly into first-, second- and third-class citizens propelled by turbines and quadruple-expansion marine engines – the magnificent achievements of modern science! And the audience hope that Jack and Rose's passionate but doomed love across the class boundaries prophetically represents the sign of a better future for humanity which will blossom from the wreck of the old 'modern' world. One of the most poignant moments in the film comes when Rose finally commits the priceless 'Heart of the Ocean' jewel to the deep.[13] Is this what film-goers and marine archaeologists alike are searching for? A variant of Jesus' priceless pearl of Matthew 13? Whether that may be or not, the story of the *Titanic* reminds us all of how fragile life is on earth, and how intimately it is bound up with nature.

What will the new millennium hold? That depends on what we learn from the parable of the *Titanic* which has been played out through the history of the twentieth century. In this, the deep seems to throw into question the very assumptions on which a proud civilization has been built. Each society creates or receives its own mythology to make sense of life, and to give it a sense of values and purpose. Today's myth is still rooted in a mechanistic way of thinking which denies or represses spirituality. It has been embraced by popular vote ever since Darwin and the Church clashed over the *Origin of Species*, and the Church lost. Having disposed of one great story which gave coherence to human life, Western culture substituted another called scientific progress. This myth is proving to be shot through with holes. The twentieth century has brought humankind to the edge of the abyss many times. Scientific technology cannot save the world from itself. When Carl Jung wrote his great book

Modern Man in Search of a Soul[14] two generations ago, he gave us a prophetic anticipation of this millennial crisis for Western civilization. Only a new myth, he predicted, which could bring it new spiritual resources could bring renewal of life and hope. At the beginning of a new millennium, the search is on in earnest . . .

God in the depths of tragedy?

The *Titanic* tragedy points to a further series of questions beyond the question of blame for the tragedy at the time, raised too by the reaction to the sinking of the *Estonia*, and every other similar disaster involving pointless loss of life and lasting pain. As the liner went down, the ship's band were reported to have been playing the hymn 'Nearer my God to thee'. Every member of the band was drowned. Was their faith misplaced? Where *was* God when the great liner foundered? Was the sinking simply a chance of fate using the instrument of the cruel sea? Or was the sea that night somehow an instrument of God's judgement on Western civilization, arrogant and over-confident in its ability to determine its future? If so, was it a final judgement on the lives of those who were swallowed up in its waters? Or was there a future for them beyond death? Does the nature and action of the sea, with its physical expressions of chaos, darkness and depth, mean that all human life is doomed to futility?

To us it is not given
in any place to rest;
suffering humanity
perishes and falls
haphazardly from one
hour to the other,
like water dashed
from crag to crag.
Year after year, down into the unknown.[15]

Or does the symbolism of the sea, with all its sense of adventure, potential and indeed embodiment of birth and the sustenance of life itself, give us a clue, despite all the pain and suffering, to the presence and purpose of God at work within his creation?

Chapter 3

CHARTING THE WAYS OF THE DEEP

God moves in a mysterious way
his wonders to perform;
he plants his footsteps in the sea,
and rides upon the storm.[1]

No nation on earth has a more turbulent and tragic history than the Jewish people. Their experience qualifies them well to give us a theological term for the reality and experience of the deep. It is called in Hebrew *tehom*, the dark chaotic primeval watery mass out of which creation is born. This theological strand runs like a river through the whole Bible, and starts where earth's history starts in the geological record, with an all-embracing ocean.

> In the beginning when God began to create the heavens and the earth, the earth was a formless void and darkness covered the face of the deep, while the spirit of God swept over the face of the waters.
>
> (Genesis 1.1–2)

From the start, here is a God who is constantly at work, creating and re-creating from the raw material at his disposal. The traditional translation, 'God created the heavens and the earth', gives the impression that God's job in creation was finished once he had made the universe and set it going. For most of the Christian era, the givenness and stability of creation has been assumed, until the last two centuries, when discoveries of modern science and environmental issues have called this into question. Through the Bible, the persistent symbol of the deep points to a continuous creative process in history. Every branch of science too points to continuous creation and re-creation, whether among the galaxies at the farthest corner of the universe, or in the tiniest living cell. The meaning of the word 'create' in Genesis 1 suggests the patient work of a craftsman, lovingly bringing the potential and best possibilities out of all that he makes.

The writer intends us to understand that the whole universe is always in his hands as he fashions and re-fashions his material.

What then does the divine potter have to work on? The precise meaning of the words and their relationship to each other at the beginning of creation is unclear.[2] Formless void translates two Hebrew words, *tohu wa-bohu*. *Tohu* implies a formless state of 'non-being' of matter, while *bohu* has the feeling of a wild empty desert, all mysteriously wrapped up together under a layer of thick darkness. The *tehom*, or 'deep', appears to undergird and at the same time be identified with the *tohu wa-bohu*. This third ingredient of primeval uncreated matter is a chaotic dark watery waste, over which the Spirit of God roars like a mighty storm wind. Sailors know only too well how wind and water belong together! Joseph Conrad observes these features of *tehom* as well as its antiquity in *The Mirror of the Sea*.

> If you would know the age of the earth, look upon the sea in a storm. The greyness of the whole immense surface, the wind furrows upon the faces of the waves, the great masses of foam, tossed about and waving like matted white locks, give to the sea in a gale an appearance of hoary age, lustreless, dull, without gleams, as though it had been created before light itself.[3]

These three constituent elements of uncreated matter – empty barren incoherence, watery depths and darkness – are now subject to the mysterious motions of the wind of the Spirit illustrating two aspects of God's creative action. The force of the gale represents immense life and power to bring the universe into being. The fluttering or hovering of the Spirit, which is also implied, paradoxically indicates infinite gentle care. God's mother-eagle-like concern for Israel in their epic wilderness journey across their own *tohu wa-bohu*, to be created as a nation through the experience of the desert, is later described in a similar fashion.

> He sustained him in a desert land, in a howling wilderness waste;
> he shielded him, cared for him, guarded him as the apple of his eye.
> As an eagle stirs up its nest and hovers over its young;
> as it spreads its wings, takes them up, and bears them aloft on
> its pinions,
> the Lord alone guided him . . .
>
> (Deuteronomy 32.10–12)

Before land appears, we are told that God created light, which is described as altogether good, and separated light from darkness. This whole process sounds magnificently sonorous in Hebrew poetry, but rather prosaic in English translation. We need music here rather than words! In Haydn's visionary oratorio *The Creation*, the orchestral prelude represents the *tohu wa-bohu* and *tehom* combining 'apparent irreconcilables – terseness with spaciousness, a sense of formlessness and lawlessness (produced by purely musical means, distant modulations and the cancelling out of an implied tonality by contradictory harmonies), with a strong inner unity of design'.[4] There is a marvellous moment shortly after when the chorus, beginning quietly over a hushed pulsating accompaniment representing the movement of the Spirit, suddenly blasts the word 'light' in a brilliant C major key, making a sharp contrast with the grey ambiguity before.

Darkness is not described as 'good' here, in the same way that light is. God names them both, recognizing that darkness has a right to exist along with light, and that he is in control of both. We are not told where darkness comes from any more than the *tehom* over which the Spirit of God broods and roars. The implication is that chaos, emptiness and darkness are intimately linked in human experience with what we have identified as the depths. They are 'non-being' out of which, in God's hands, things 'become'.

To create the heavens and the earth, the land and the seas, God splits the primordial *tehom* into two great areas, one above the heavens, and another below the dome of the sky. Out of the latter, land and sea are formed, the seas and rivers being residual drops of 'deep' left over and channelled in the creative process. Figure 1 sketches the ancient three-decker cosmology common to Old and New Testaments. Genesis 1 has often been compared with the Babylonian account of creation to which it bears a superficial resemblance. The Babylonian story begins with an internecine battle between the gods of the sweet and salt-water oceans and their offspring. This ends with Tiamat (or Rahab), the chaotic salt-water goddess, being split in two by Marduk, and her corpse stretched out to form the cosmos. The Hebrews who gave us Genesis were well aware of these ancient Near-Eastern sagas but give them a very different twist. In the beginning a good God creates a good and moral universe. The Bible beginning is a beautiful, purposeful design, bringing order out of chaos. Indeed, at the end of the week of creation,

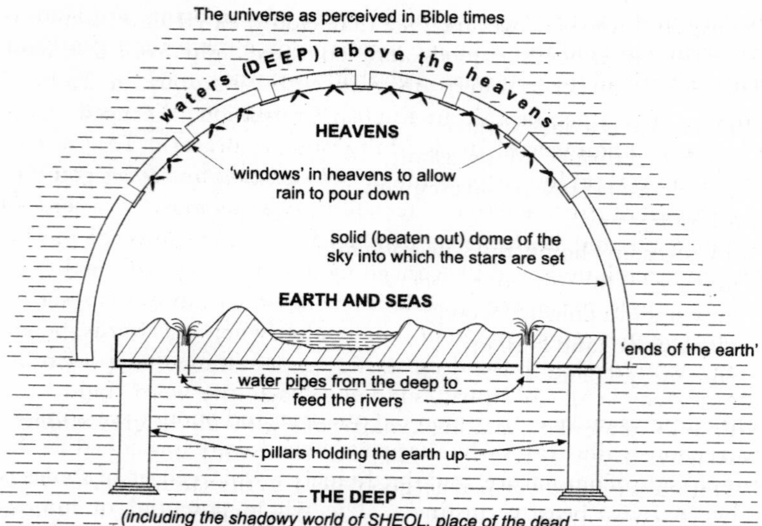

Figure 1 The universe as perceived in Bible Times

> God saw everything that he had made, and indeed, it was very good . . .
>
> Thus the heavens and the earth were finished, and all their multitude. And on the seventh day, God finished the work that he had done, and he rested . . .
>
> (Genesis 1.31—2.1)

God completes his grand design by resting himself – but this is not the end of the creation story, just the end of the beginning. The good creation still includes the deep with its sea monsters, theological representations of the original monster of chaos. Their mention leads us to recognize that 'even the powers of evil maintain their freedom to sport in the ordered realm of God's and nature's ocean. Even they are good for God's plan.'[5] So the deep, with its teeming life at once playful and sinister, is always there to be worked on unceasingly by the creative gale of the Spirit, as the course of history is played out.

The slippery slope to the Flood

The parable of the Fall shows us only too clearly that the deep is there, not just in the natural world, but in every human being. For God to create humankind in his image means to give them their powerful self-will with all the potential to go their own way.

> The world is a dark surface,
> a polished surface aslant, aslant,
> a world aslant towards Auschwitz,
> aslant my town,
> my town, my home, my wife and child
> high up on the thin edge – below,
> only smooth polished wood,
> black wood, and high up
> you, me, all of us[6]

The cunning snake with its pointed question and phoney reassurance marvellously illustrates what happens when we are torpedoed by the animal side of our nature, and the divinely given freedom of choice is subverted by 'beastly' instincts. The whole potential of human beings is to be human. Our whole vocation is to transcend the baser instincts of the animal world and be stewards and not spoilers of creation.

The awful results of human rebellion against God are spelt out in these early chapters of Genesis. The parable of the Flood acts as a climax to the increasing free rein of evil and violence marking human relationships, and the effect this has on the natural world. Human beings have themselves been responsible for bringing chaos and pain back to a world of ordered beauty. And God is sorry. 'He experiences in his own heart, what we living men and women, made in his image experience in our hearts. Such a view is very different from the theology of the epic poems of the Near East which may provide the framework for what follows. In these, we have a conflict *between the gods*. Here in Genesis we have a conflict *within the one God* . . . God by his own free choice necessarily suffers for the sin of man.'[7] The implication is that as part of the ongoing creative process, God is so intimately involved with the consequences of human rebellion that he suffers alongside human beings, and acts redemptively *within* the situation where evil seems to have run totally out of control. The same pattern occurs in the Gospel account of the incarnation and the cross. Humanity's total rebellion necessarily involves God's total judgement, which means nothing less than a reversal of the whole original process of creation back to chaos. And the symbolism of the deep has a key role to play in this drama, because it is both a picture of sin, the barren disintegration (*tohu*) and chaos that human beings have willed upon themselves, and its awful consequences.

As the insects, birds and animals troop into the ark it is as though the reel of film that was shown at the beginning is being run backwards. With one difference. Noah walks with God. In Noah, God has found a man of integrity to whom he can confidently trust his original purpose for creation. His very name is ambiguously translated as 'comfort' and 'rest'. In Noah's obedience God could find comfort that despite the appalling havoc brought on creation through unbridled human wickedness, his original good plan would not be totally lost to the deep. In Noah and his ark, God could rest, knowing that everything he had made would after all have a future. So it was that:

> In the six-hundredth year of Noah's life . . . all the fountains of the great deep burst forth, and the windows of the heavens were opened.
>
> (Genesis 7.11)

We must notice here that these waters above the heavens now let loose were not just rain-clouds. These depths *above* are part of the cosmic structure. What is described here is not just a local flood around the Tigris and Euphrates basin. This is a universal catastrophe. 'When the heavenly ocean breaks forth upon the earth below, and the primaeval sea beneath the earth, which is restrained by God, not freed from its bonds gushes up through yawning chasms onto the earth, there is a destruction of the entire cosmic system.'[8] And the future of the universe now rests entirely with the contents of the ark bobbing around on top of the water.

When the land is totally scoured clean from evil by the waters, God remembers Noah's faithfulness and restrains the flood-waters. The ark comes to 'rest' on Ararat, the highest mountain known to the world then. God then liberates the survivors from the chaos which has threatened them, and gives them a fresh start. Humanity could never again claim that the earth was there just to do what they liked with. The story of the Flood is an archetypal paradigm of God's judgement and grace, with the deep as its instrument.

Timeless parables

What sort of writing is this? It cannot be scientific, literal, 'factual' in the sense that modern minds understand things. For one thing, God is the centre of the narrative, and that is hardly scientific in the conventional sense. These words were not written to give us a clue about the way the world was made so that we could set it alongside other scientific theories of origins. They are simply about God's purposes in fashioning the cosmos. For another, the language is pictorial: each name, each story is pregnant with meaning about the Almighty, the human condition, and the relationship people ought to have with their God and with the natural world. For example, the ark is not a 'real' boat in the scientific sense. One man and his three sons could never build a craft more than half the length of the *Titanic* in a relatively short time for a start. No, the ark was a 'theological' boat, real in a different sense, echoed in other parts of the Bible as well.

At the beginning of Genesis we have a series of wonderful parables with a timeless message for people everywhere, set in the midst of a strange anachronistic three-decker universe. These stories are often written in verse, because they are poetry. Sometimes they use the mythic symbols of the ancient Near East, because this was the most descriptive way then known to express human understanding of the origin and meaning of life. Sometimes they echo time-honoured memories of widespread flooding in the region following the end of the last ice age. Whatever literary form they take, it is essential we *resist* the temptation to demythologize them in an attempt to accommodate them to modern 'scientific' thought patterns. If we can live with the embarrassment of the three-decker picture the Bible presents us with, we have a rich seam of theological truth to mine: truth that fires our imagination, gives meaning to our worship and prayer, and makes profound sense of our human experience.[9] This is how we understand 'the depths' here, and this is the motive for the rest of our exploration.

Stories of hope for desperate times

The parables of Genesis 1–11 are woven together from two great literary traditions. One written source dates from the early years of the Monarchy in the ninth to tenth centuries BCE, incorporating an emphasis on the southern, last remaining, Kingdom of Judah. The other relates history and pre-history to ethical and ritual precepts, and although containing some of the oldest aural tradition in the Bible, dates in its final form from after the exile in Babylon was over.[10] It is difficult to imagine the agonizing sense of 'non-being' and God-forsakenness felt by the refugees on the banks of the Euphrates following the rape of their 'land of milk and honey' and the destruction of Jerusalem in 587 BCE. The trauma of the exile focused attention on the oral and written traditions of the Jews: it had to, if any of what was precious to them, and identified them as a distinct people, was to survive. Nebuchadnezzar could take away their king, their temple, and their land, but he could not take away their memories or their sacred scriptures.

These traditions lived in their hearts as well as written records, and gave them hope when it seemed that God had judged them and abandoned them to their fate, far from home. Adam and Eve, Cain and Abel, Enoch, and Noah and his family took on a whole new meaning for the survivors on the banks of the Euphrates. After all, that's where Creation all started. And the images of Noah, the man who walked with God, faithful and obedient to his voice amid the sexual excesses and violence of the antediluvian world, standing firm against the taunts of his neighbours as he built the ark, gave them a role model as a people for the future. Hearing and obeying God's voice would always be the answer to the threatening *tehom*.

And the ark itself – why, this was a picture of a little community far from its homeland on earth, protected and nurtured by God himself, preserving all that was good for the future of humankind! After the land had been cleaned by the flood, it was ready for occupation again and a new beginning. Everything made sense. God had not forgotten after all. But he was not a tribal God, like the gods whose rise and fall fluctuated with the political fortunes of the nations round about. The Jewish people discovered they had no claim on God except what he revealed himself to be. And their calling was to share him with the rest of the world, because he was none other than Lord of the cosmos:

> Have you not known, have you not heard?
> Has it not been told you from the beginning?
> Have you not understood from the foundations of the earth?
> It is he who sits above the circle of the earth,
> and its inhabitants are like grasshoppers;

who stretches out the heavens like a curtain,
and spreads them like a tent to live in;
who brings princes to naught,
and makes the rulers of the earth as nothing
. . . To whom then will you compare me,
or who is my equal? says the Holy One.
Lift up your eyes and see:
Who created these?

(Isaiah 40.21–3, 25–6)

This combination of old traditions really made sense to the exiles. A new outburst of prophecy reminded them that after all the Spirit of the true God was to be found with them in the deep. Far from defeat, the exile was a vindication of his justice and might over hostile powers. Far from land, king and temple, their Lord could still speak – and in awesome clarity:

Awake, awake, put on strength, O arm of the Lord!
Awake, as in days of old, the generations of long ago!
Was it not you who cut Rahab in pieces, who pierced the dragon?
Was it not you who dried up the sea, the waters of the great deep;
who made the depths of the sea a way for the redeemed to cross over?
So the ransomed of the Lord shall return, and come to Zion with singing;
everlasting joy shall be upon their heads;
they shall obtain joy and gladness, and sorrow and sighing shall flee away.

(Isaiah 51.9–11)

In this word of hope for the future, the prophet brilliantly links mythological symbols of creation with the historic story of the first Exodus from Pharaoh's clutches in Egypt. He expects God to act in exactly the same way in the place where Marduk is supposed to be king. At the first Exodus, the deep becomes a birth canal of dry ground from which the Hebrew community was born into a new world of freedom and opportunity via the wilderness of Sinai. God triumphs over the power of the deep, now represented by Pharaoh's armies.

Then the Lord said to Moses . . . 'Tell the Israelites to go forward.

But you lift up your staff, and stretch out your hand over the sea and divide it, that the Israelites may go into the sea on dry ground.
(Exodus 14.15–16)

The theologians of Israel make a clear connection with the events surrounding the creation of the cosmos. Or perhaps it is the other way about. The best theology is fashioned through hard experience. As they reflect on the way the nation was created through the waters, they catch a vision of God's original purposes in creation. Only now, as the creator fights his battles with the recalcitrant deep in the form of hostile political powers, the theme of struggle spills over into the original serene creation imagery.

Yet God my King is from of old, working salvation in the earth.
You divided the sea by your might; you broke the heads of the
dragons in the waters.
You crushed the heads of Leviathan; you gave him as food for the
creatures of the wilderness.
You cut openings for springs and torrents; you dried up
ever-flowing streams.
Yours is the day, yours also the night; you established the
luminaries and the sun.
You have fixed all the bounds of the earth; you made summer and
winter.

(Psalm 74.12–17)

A pretty comprehensive victory when the desert jackals are fed pieces of the ancient sea-monster! The exiles had only a short time to wait for God's promises. The first survivors went back just forty years after their exile, a mirror of those first forty years of wandering in the Sinai desert. In 539 BCE, the Persian armies occupied Babylon and, shortly after, released the Jews, who drifted back in small parties west and then south to their homeland. There, they found another kind of deep, the *tohu wa-bohu* variety yet again, a virtually uninhabited wasteland where once there was a thriving community.[11] But it was a time for new beginnings. The deep would always be there, and there is no other way for the redeemed but the re-creation of a new nation, a restored land, and a renewed faith through this harrowing experience of the depths.

Rebirthing the images

Right through the Bible, images of the deep, monsters and all, on occasions, become represented in an imaginative, but imprecise way in historic events and naturally occurring features like seas, floods, rivers, deserts and the dark. This way, in which the continuously creating and re-creating God makes theology contemporary, relevant and practical as people experience his ways in their lives, reaches its climax in the book of Revelation. At each stage in the unfolding of the story, these images are reborn. So Moses, in his miraculous nurture as a baby, becomes another symbol of the grace of God, preparing the way for him to grow up as a great leader and saviour of his people from the oppressive power of Pharaoh's regime.

> The daughter of Pharaoh came down to bathe at the river . . . She saw the basket among the reeds and sent her maid to bring it. When she opened it, she saw the child. He was crying, and she took pity on him.
>
> (Exodus 2.5–6)

And the same word is used for Moses' basket floating helplessly among the reeds, as for Noah's ark! Much later, the deep in the form of the river Nile becomes personified as the oppressive power of a later Egyptian government, the monster sea snake, which has to be dealt with as at the beginning:

> On that day the Lord with his cruel and great and strong sword will punish Leviathan the fleeing serpent, Leviathan the twisting serpent, and he will kill the dragon that is in the sea.
>
> (Isaiah 27.1)

The geography of the Nile, snaking through the desert, adds to the water/wasteland symbolism, suggesting the dragon inhabiting the desert as it flows north to the Mediterranean for hundreds of miles from its source in Ethiopia.

In the parable of Jonah, the prophet's disobedience stirs up the deep to endanger the lives of his fellow seafarers. One person's disobedience can have awful social consequences for many other innocent people. Jonah volunteers to be thrown overboard as a sacrifice to the deep in order for them to survive. In answer to the prayers of the sailors (an interesting example of the effectiveness of the prayers of those of another faith), God demonstrates his control over the deep by turning the fierce 'dragon' residing there into a large friendly fish. After three days and nights Jonah is thrown up onto dry land to give him a second chance to obey God's command. A 'death' and 'rebirth' in God's hands! When he reaches Nineveh, he is confronted by the desert, another form of the deep and a new test to his faith and generosity of spirit.

This story belongs to the same family of sagas as Noah and the ark, although it comes from a much later period in Jewish history. In 'Jonah', the 'ark', which is the instrument of God's grace, is not a boat but a kind of *living submarine*, keeping him safe. 'Jonah' is written as a story about one individual. But it is about a people. *Yonah*, which means 'dove', is one of the names for Israel in the Psalms. Jonah son of *Amittai*, or 'truth', represents the people of Israel who have consistently refused to take the message of God's mercy to their gentile neighbours, whom he loves just as much. This unusual 'prophecy' is one of the clearest Old Testament preparations for the New Testament gospel. It dramatically links all three of the 'depth' elements we have identified: *the chaotic waters, the desert, and cosmic darkness*, which here is identified with the place of the dead, in this case, the experience of exile:[12]

> The waters closed in over me; the deep surrounded me;
> weeds were wrapped around my head at the roots of the mountains.
> I went down to the land whose bars closed upon me forever;
> yet you brought up my life from the Pit, O Lord my God.
>
> (Jonah 2.5–6)

Such an experience points forward to the New Testament and the theme of resurrection, where God is with his people even in the deepest of depths and can redeem them from deepest darkness. Now there is nowhere he cannot be.

> Where can I go from your spirit? Or where can I flee from your presence?
> If I ascend to heaven, you are there; if I make my bed in Sheol, you are there.
>
> (Psalm 139.7–8)

The depths in the Gospel story

Before the beginning of Jesus' public ministry, the Synoptic evangelists bring together the mighty Spirit and the awesome deep as they announce the new creation God is bringing to the earth in the story of his baptism and testing in the wilderness. By contrast, John's Gospel begins by consciously imitating Genesis 1, with the imagery of the Word in creation. The deep is present throughout his Gospel in the presence of the cosmic darkness. The powers of the deep are the 'world' (*kosmos*) of Jewish and Roman religious and political power acting in opposition to Jesus the eternal light. Those who belong to the opposition, whose beliefs are quite sorted out and seek to impose their own particular world view to maintain the status quo, are shown to be truly 'in the dark' as they fail to recognize who he is, and the truth of his message.

The setting of the Gospels includes a deep lake, the 'sea' of Galilee at its heart, 210 metres below sea level. This physical representation of the *tehom* forms a backcloth to much of Jesus' teaching and actions, especially in the Synoptic Gospels. He calls his first fishermen disciples by the seashore, and encourages them to *put out into deep water* to be participants in his new creation as they follow him (Luke 5.4). As a preface to his seminal teaching in parables we read:

> Again he began to teach beside the sea. Such a very large crowd gathered around him that he got into a boat on the sea and sat there, while the whole crowd was beside the sea on the land. He began to teach them many things . . .
>
> (Mark 4.1–2)

Here is the 'ark' again, commanded by Jesus, a latter-day 'greater than Noah' who teaches the people as a 'greater than Moses', using the boat as a pulpit, floating offshore with the crowd on the water's edge. The message of the Kingdom is that they must leave behind the ways of a doomed sectarian Jewish civilization. If they take to heart what Jesus teaches them they will have to leave the shore, and go with him as members of the 'true Israel' through the waters.

The Gospels spell out what this means in an amazing kaleidoscope of 'depth' imagery to which we shall return again later. Mark continues with the famous scene where the disciples are with Jesus on the lake, the primal gale roars once more, and the waves of the *tehom* rise up to threaten their lives. As he stills the storm, Jesus demonstrates the presence and power of the God of creation. His next mighty work is to quell the storm in the life of a possessed man, sending his evil spirits back to the deep, where they belong. This is shortly followed by the picture of Jesus walking on the water, while every Gospel goes on to tell the story of the miraculous feeding in the desert, carrying faint echoes of Psalm 74, referred to above. And the Sermon on the Mount, Jesus' great Kingdom manifesto, ends with the following challenge, reminding his hearers of the symbolism of the Genesis flood:

> Everyone then who hears these words of mine and acts on them will be like a wise man who built his house on rock. The rain fell, the floods came, and the winds blew and beat on that house, but it did not fall, because it had been founded on rock.
>
> (Matthew 7.24–5)

The *tehom* above and below, and the safe 'ark' of Noah's flood, are all here again, with that same call to hear the word and obey it, just as Noah did – in order to find life through riding out the deep! It is *on this rock* that Christ will build his Church, and the powers of the deep, this time represented by the deadly darkness of *the gates of Hades*, will never prevail against it (Mathew 16.18).

Towards the climax of the Synoptic Gospels, Jesus prophesies the next wholesale destruction of Jerusalem by the overwhelming flood of the Roman invading armies. Here is a dramatic New Testament reminder to the people of Judaea of the instability of the deep, and its potential to engulf them in its chaos yet again if they reject his ways:

> . . . Jerusalem will be trampled on by the Gentiles, until the times of the Gentiles are fulfilled. There will be signs in the sun, the moon, and the stars, and on the earth distress among nations confused by the roaring of the sea and the waves. People will faint from fear and foreboding of what is coming upon the world, for the powers of the heavens will be shaken.
>
> (Luke 21.24–6)

In all four Gospels the battle between the light and darkness reaches its greatest intensity in the suffering and crucifixion of Jesus Christ, when for a moment the *tehom* appears to have won, in Jesus' cry of God-forsakenness in the darkness on the cross (Mark 15.33–4). How appropriate then for John to illustrate the truth of Christ's victory over darkness and death with a resurrection breakfast by that old familiar 'sea', and a renewed commission to follow Jesus come what may (John 21.1–21). Jesus Christ may have won the decisive battle with the darkness, but in the life of his disciples of every age, the *tehom* is a force still to be reckoned with.

In Paul's teaching, the deep is notably represented by the motif of the fallen cosmic powers. This is why it is the sea which very nearly prevents the good news of Jesus being taken by Paul to Rome, the focus of first-century political power and dominance. One day there will be no more *tehom* (Revelation 21.1), because such a mighty power will be redeemed and its water will be channelled into the river of life. But for now the battle is fierce:

> We were being pounded by the storm so violently that on the next day they began to throw the cargo overboard ... When neither sun nor stars appeared for many days, and no small tempest raged, all hope of our being saved was at last abandoned ... Paul then stood up ... 'keep up your courage, men, for I have faith in God that it will be exactly as I have been told.'
>
> (Acts 27.18–21, 25)

Paul's shipwreck and rescue occupies exactly the same point in Acts as does the cross and resurrection in Luke. Such experiences must have encouraged him to elaborate the sentiments of Psalm 139 so that he could joyfully exclaim:

> In all these things we are more than conquerors through him who loved us. For I am convinced that neither death, nor life, nor angels, nor rulers, nor things present, nor things to come, nor powers, nor height, nor depth, nor anything else in all creation, will be able to separate us from the love of God in Christ Jesus our Lord.[13]
>
> (Romans 8.37–9)

Chapter 4

The Deep in the Journey of Life

Be adored among men,
God, three-numberèd form;
Wring thy rebel, dogged in den,
Man's malice, with wrecking and storm.
Beyond saying sweet, past telling of tongue,
Thou art lightning and love, I found it, a winter and warm;
Father and fondler of heart thou hast wrung:
Hast thy dark descending and most art merciful then. [1]

The Bible describes people like a miniature cosmos – a unity of body, mind and spirit. The chaotic waters of the deep hang over and underlie the earth, held back by the mercy and love of the creator, and the promises to humankind after the flood. They occur too in the hearts and lives of men and women. In this private cosmos, God is building and refashioning all that he is making. How often we are tempted to undo his handiwork through our own wilfulness, blindness and ignorance when we try to pursue the adventure of life without reference to him!

We can think of God's character-building like the constant process of mountain-building and the formation and refashioning of the morphology of the earth through tectonic movements, the endless ferment of molten magma underneath the earth's crust, and the action of wind, rain, sea and human activity above it all. Sometimes these processes take a long time, but even small movements have earth-changing long-term effects. A global sea-level rise of 3 metres in the next hundred years may not seem very much measured against the rocks on an average English beach, but the effects it could have for the millions of people living at sea level could be colossal. In our own spiritual development, steady, significant long-term life-changes often occur too slowly to notice. On the other hand sudden unexpected catastrophes throw us off balance like earthquakes and volcanic eruptions, and make us feel our lives are being turned upside-down, never to be the same again.

In human terms our reactions to life-changing forces within and beyond us are most violent when our skin is thinnest, our wounds are tenderest and our feelings are fiercest. It is at this time we take the blows in either silence or apology – out of propriety or habit we bury our thoughts and feelings deeper down in self-reproach or depression. Or we explode with unexpected and uncharacteristic violence with the magma of hot anger and indignation welling up inside us, pouring out and touching those nearest and often dearest to us. 'I don't know what got into me!', we exclaim. Which is surprising when we are trying to explain something which has clearly come from deep within us, even though it might have been triggered off by an apparently unconnected event or remark on the surface.

As the earth evolves, and the continents rearrange themselves over the aeons of time, one thing is certain. The seas will always be there. And the creation of significant new land takes place on the edge of continents, where earthquakes take place, where the volcanoes are exploding, where deep sub-crustal movements are moving deeper, and where the ocean floor splits into fathomless canyons. At the same time, in these places of instability and growth, the soil is most fertile. Volcanic ash makes a marvellous basis for rich, productive loam! Human life shows similar features. If we are willing to live 'on the edge', to accept challenges, to honestly face the murky deep within our innermost souls, we shall grow in character and maturity. Our lives will bear fruit and we may find God at the heart of all the upheaval.

In the last chapter we identified three features about the raw material from which the universe was fashioned at the beginning, and continues to be formed. This primal stuff, represented within the ideas contained in the poetic Hebrew words *tohu wa-bohu* and *tehom*, we have identified as *chaotic waters, barren desert, and deep darkness*. All three feature in the Bible as part of the stuff of human experience.

Chaotic waters

In the beginning God overcame the power of the dark primal deep. Though that victory was won in the beginning, the roar of Israel's enemies was ever-present both at their borders and within their hearts. The chaotic waters of the deep represented the threat they constantly posed. The promised land was a good place to be, a place of well-being and security where everyone had their own vine and fig tree, and the yearly pattern of pastoral life and religious festivals could be celebrated with joy. The return of the deep meant the complete opposite of all that. Disruption of the fabric of national life, threats to family, land and property. Political and social confusion, and emotional turmoil within. The draining of mental and physical strength which might come from fighting and sinking in a wild sea, physically and spiritually.

> Save me, O God, for the waters have come up to my neck.
> I sink in deep mire, where there is no foothold;
> I have come into deep waters, and the flood sweeps over me.
> (Psalm 69.1–2)

The Israelites, landlubbers at heart, feared the whole ordered world could return to chaos again. The 'windows of heaven' shut up after Noah's flood, and the fountains of the deep that brought it about as well, could once more open up. The people of God learnt through hard experience that if they journeyed on, walking in partnership with God, they would be safe. Rebelling against him and going their own way would risk another encounter with the deep.

> Out of the depths I cry to you, O Lord. Lord, hear my voice!
> If you, O Lord, should mark iniquities, Lord, who could stand?
> But there is forgiveness with you, so that you may be revered.
> (Psalm 130.1, 3–4)

Taming the waters

At the beginning of all things, each act of creation produced a little more order and beauty out of the chaos. The water that remained represented a challenge to the ordered world that God was creating. The world needed water for life. So the Hebrews saw God's power at work, channelling the *tehom* into springs, streams, rivers, lakes and sea to refresh humans and animals alike. So, through Moses, God refreshed the people and their animals through the 'many waters' which gushed out from the rock (Numbers 20.11). The next stage of their journey of faith was determined by the next oasis on the way. Psalm 29 by contrast celebrates God's enthronement *above* the heavens and earth in the control he exercises over the thunder, lightning and rainstorm to bring to birth and sustain life. As the *tehom* thundered and did its work, everybody in the temple shouted glory, in approval! So the chaotic sea has an ambivalent character as well, like the sea, its visible expression. It can threaten, but it can also renew the bodies as well as the spirits of God's people. The prophet looks forward to the day once more when

> waters shall break forth in the wilderness, and streams in the desert;
> the burning sand shall become a pool, and the thirsty ground
> springs of water;
>
> (Isaiah 35.6–7)

Human tears can illustrate one way the deep is visibly channelled to represent sacramentally the movement of God within human experience. If the advancing waters drive us personally back to God in repentance and anger or through distress or bereavement, then surely it is reasonable we should expect such a sign. It is common to speak of being overcome with floods of tears. This is not far from the language of the Psalms, where the flood can come up from within, as well as from external circumstances.

> Every night I flood my bed with tears; I drench my couch with
> my weeping.
> My eyes waste away because of grief; they grow weak because of all
> my foes.
>
> (Psalm 6.6–7)

Tears can be evidence of the depth of emotion, along with verbal expressions of feelings of sorrow, bitterness or indeed joy. They can be positively cathartic and refreshing as well, releasing tension and taking people 'out of themselves', especially when they are 'beyond words'. Tears can also represent sympathy, fellowship and concern for others, 'weeping with those who weep'. I remember a woman in my congregation once who was very anxious because she could not pray in tongues. It was not long before I discovered she had a marvellous gift of tears in her praying for others. There was no doubt of the movement of the Holy Spirit in the depth of her life! Mystic theology sees the effect of tears as purifying and enlightening the soul, a sign of the living water of the Spirit flowing from the heart.[2]

Barren desert

Israel was always sandwiched geographically between the deep sea and the barren wilderness. Although the land east and south of Palestine was not true desert, it was still barren, rocky, inhospitable and infertile, a haunt for wild jackals and other scavengers. The Dead Sea, sat there right in the path of the advancing pilgrims, was many hundreds of metres below sea level, a permanent and eloquent sign of this strange trinity of the deep, desert waste, and death wrapped up in a single package!

The desert experience was burned deep into the Jewish psyche, ever since at the time of the Exodus they had taken forty years to travel 70 miles as the crow flies. It does not take much imagination to appreciate what that means in terms of wandering round in circles. There are no paths in the desert except the one we make ourselves! When later they crossed the Jordan and settled down, memories of this awful wilderness formed an indelible image within them, reinforced by the readings and communal experience of the yearly festivals of Passover and Tabernacles.

Desert for the Jews meant a vast unmanageable parched waterless place of poverty, failure, impotence and loneliness. It could be any place of interminable tedious routine, of disappointment, a place where they came to the end of their own resources, and a place of spiritual dryness. Many of the great Old Testament heroes had first-hand experience of the power of the desert: Abraham, Isaac, Jacob, Joseph, Moses, Caleb, Joshua, Elijah, Jeremiah, Job and Jonah. In the New Testament, John the Baptist and St Paul learnt the hard way through the desert experience, while the desert plays a crucial role in the experience and teaching of Jesus Christ. The great psalms recalling salvation history (78, 105, 106 and 136) testify to the nation's experience of the desert; the replies of Job to his comforters, and several psalms, bear personal testimony to the inner feelings of sufferers undergoing the rigours of the desert experience which modern pilgrims know only too well:

My heart is stricken and withered like grass;
I am too wasted to eat my bread.
I am like an owl of the wilderness,
like a little owl of the waste places.

I lie awake;
I am like a lonely bird on the housetop.
(Psalm 102.4, 6–7)

In that experience we may experience God's judgement, where we are stripped of all pretending and hiding behind all that much over-rated human self-sufficiency. In the judgement, there is revelation – of the real truth of our own poverty. The clutter we carry around with us to justify ourselves is shown up to be the pathetic baggage it really is. We are forced to face the honest truth about ourselves before God. Here we can acknowledge that we are sinners, naked, in need of rescue. Here we have to travel light, and follow the way he shows us, because there is nowhere else to go.

The place of discovery and adventure

The desert is also a place of another kind of revelation. In the clear air of the desert we can perceive God's presence more easily. This was very much the experience of those first Israelites. It was as they crossed the Red Sea that they first caught a glimpse of the power of their God to control the deep. It was as they enjoyed the water and food he provided in the desert that they began to appreciate his compassion. It was in the mighty theophany at Mount Sinai that they first heard his word of life. And it was in the pillar of cloud by day, and the fire by night, that they first saw his glory. It will be so for us too, wherever and whenever we become aware of the wilderness deep within and respond to the moving of his Spirit there. In the desert there was failure, going back, compromise and betrayal. There must have been many times when Moses thought the people were taking three steps back for every two steps forward. Progress was so slow. But God was so gentle and compassionate, as he will be with us too, when we are willing to take the next step on the adventure of faith.

Commenting on the wilderness journey, Kosuke Koyama refers to the 'three-mile-an-hour God' who walks with us, and teaches us patiently. He remarks that God's speed is a different kind of speed from the technological speed to which we are accustomed. He calls it a 'spiritual speed', going on in the depths of our lives whether we notice it or not. He sees the wilderness as a place of danger and promise – an educational situation for God's people. 'When danger and promise come together to us, it is called crisis. The Bible does not simply speak of danger. If it did so, the biblical faith would be reduced to a "protection-from-danger-religion". The Bible does not simply speak about promise. If it did so, the biblical faith would be reduced to a "happy-ending-religion".'[3] In the wilderness we are called to go beyond "protection-from-danger-religion" and "happy-ending-religion". There we are called to trust in God.

From barrenness to fruitfulness

Sometimes in our desert-as-deep experiences our progress is not merely slower than we want, but comes to a full stop altogether. Koyama speaks of the cross in this way. 'Jesus Christ came. He walked towards the "full stop". He lost his mobility. He was nailed down! What can be slower than "full stop" – nailed down? At this point of "full stop" the apostolic church proclaims that the love of God to man is ultimately and fully revealed.'[4] Jesus waited for God to vindicate him in the resurrection. We too have to wait for God to reveal his hand and learn to be patient.

> I wait for the Lord, my soul waits, and in his word I hope
>
> (Psalm 130.5)

Waiting is about growing. Any expert gardener will know all about waiting for the new growth to thrust through the cold earth after a barren winter. Any mother will know only too well the waiting and preparation time for the birth of her child. And couples who cannot seem to conceive know those barren times of waiting for fertility treatment, and the endless hospital tests once it starts, with each subsequent visit pregnant with hope. These graphic experiences of faith are paralleled in Scripture in the waiting and hoping against hope of Abraham and Sarah, Manoah and his wife, Elkanah and Hannah, Zechariah and Elizabeth, whose sterility and barrenness was transformed by the word and touch of the Lord. And Mary, whose empty womb nurtured the infant Christ through the mysterious 'overshadowing' ministry of the wings of the Holy Spirit. And the experience of those first disciples after the first Easter, when the risen Christ told them

> . . . see, I am sending upon you what my Father promised; so stay here in the city until you have been clothed with power from on high.
>
> (Luke 24.49)

Only when they had waited in that strange empty time between the

Ascension and the coming of the Holy Spirit at Pentecost could the first Church be born and exhibit new rich gifts and fruits of God's life bursting out from within them.

The alternative to progress with God

What is the alternative to encounter and progress with God in the desert? Early in the story of Genesis we meet an archetypal hard man, Cain, who after killing his brother has the nerve to complain to God that he will be hidden from his face, when all along his family have done the hiding by their own act of will. God is no debtor to anyone. He 'sends his rain upon the just and the unjust', and as a sign of his unwavering love and care, Cain receives God's mark of protection (Genesis 4.13–16). He is a classic modern tough guy as well as being an Old Testament prodigal son. After receiving that mark of God, he deliberately goes away from God's presence, settles down with his family and builds a city. But the city is in another desert place, the land of Wandering (*Nod* in Hebrew), a marvellous picture of contemporary restlessness, emptiness and longing.

The desert is not remote in southern tropics
The desert is not only round the corner
The desert is squeezed in the tube next to you
The desert is in the heart of your brother[5]

Human sin does not alter the fact that humanity bears the image of God. It will certainly distort that relationship, and cloud human vision of God. It will make God seem unnecessary or irrelevant when life is treating us kindly. When things are tough, those who resist God's spirit may experience guilt, anxiety or depression and other disconcerting effects of their inner wilderness state from time to time without in any way connecting them to the presence of God. Cain and his equivalents today might think that God, if there is such a being, is light years away 'up in heaven', but he is much nearer than they can possibly know. It is making the connection which sows seeds of faith. The mark of God is a sign of his constant grace towards humankind. It shows itself in that insatiable search for 'home' and security in property, money, status and love which can be found not 'east of Eden' but only in him; only by facing the true challenge of the desert depths.

Man is a vain thing, and man without God is a seed upon the wind:

driven this way and that, and finding no place of lodgement and germination ... crying for life beyond life, for ecstasy not of the flesh. Waste and void. Waste and void. And darkness on the face of the deep.[6]

Deep darkness

In the Bible the darkness of the deep is represented by a whole variety of physical metaphors including Death and the grave, prison and the soggy Pit, the Abyss, and Sheol or the realm of the dead. In the New Testament, this was supplemented by Gehenna, a corruption of *Ge-hinnom* (the valley of Hinnom) on the south side of Jerusalem where the city's rubbish was dumped and burnt at the time. This endlessly smouldering putrid dump became a fine symbol for the local inhabitants of the fate of the wicked in the burning fires of hell.

Common to all these metaphors is the theme of powerlessness, helplessness, hopelessness, the denial of life and sight, silence, and being forgotten. They frequently coalesce into one another, and with the other primal images of desert and sea. Each day the people of Palestine knew what it was to sink their leather buckets into the deep shafts of their rock cisterns and draw the water up. Empty cisterns were used both as graves and as prisons where captives would be bound in fetters and left to rot. There, the themes of depth, impenetrable darkness, water, abandonment, corruption and death are all present at once. The images of Sheol and the Pit effectively deconstruct all the 'being' created in human life through the brooding and blowing of the Holy Spirit over the *tehom*, and return it to the 'non-being' of dark chaos from which it began! The most famous of those who survived these 'pits' are Joseph and Jeremiah. Few of the rest were so lucky.

God in awesome dark power

Heartfelt cries from the Pit in the Bible remind us that the God who meets us in our failures and sorrows with gentleness and forgiveness is also a God who can be terrifying and shocking as well. Here the experience is not so much of the dryness and emptiness which strips us bare, but the awesome mysterious power of God who allows the deep to confront us and throw us without warning. Personal crises of health, circumstances and relationships can suddenly turn the neat, tidy and ordered lives we have built for ourselves into murky darkness. Our immediate natural inclination is to cry with the prophet,

> O that you would tear open the heavens and come down
>
> (Isaiah 64.1)

We easily forget the context and the sequel. The God we demand to come down and bring light to our darkness is the God who makes the mountains quake and the nations tremble at his presence. He is the potter, and we are the clay in his hand (Isaiah 64.1, 3, 8). He is not a matey deity who shines a flashlight into some dark corner of his recalcitrant universe on demand. He is, in Rudolf Otto's famous phrase, the God who is *mysterium tremendum et fascinans* – a holy God, even more a threat to our spiritual balance than the event which has provoked our desperate cry! There are over forty occasions when God is referred to as terrible in the Old Testament. Even such a spiritual giant as Moses is told that he cannot see God face to face, but he might see his backside if he hides in a cleft in the rock on Sinai as he passes by! In the New Testament the pattern is repeated. The blazing laser of light from heaven that stops Saul in his tracks on his way to Damascus actually causes blindness, not increased sight! When God *does* come down, revealing himself as a human being in the incarnation for all to see, he is unrecognized, and eventually crucified by the very people who claim to know God most profoundly. In fact, the blind have much better eyesight.

If we demand sight in the darkness which stops our life in its tracks, we may well find God's response in that *we*, and not so much the heavens, are opened up, and made vulnerable, stripped of our natural defences like Isaiah in his great vision in the temple as he worshipped. Our only possible response before such a personal theophany can be:

> Woe is me! I am lost, for I am a man of unclean lips, and I live among a people of unclean lips; yet my eyes have seen the King, the Lord of hosts!
>
> (Isaiah 6.5)

God's gift to Isaiah and all who would be his disciples is not so much sight as insight. Isaiah's inner consciousness and unconscious is opened up to the point where he could respond to the creative power of the Spirit of God hovering over the uncreated depths in his life, and God could do a new thing with him. This encounter meant that he had to face and own up to previously hidden and unrecognized sin in his own life, and the lives around him. It is this, as well as the awesome and terrifying vision at the time, which so disturbed him. Yet this moment of truth became life-changing, maturing, character-forming in a way Isaiah could never imagine. A seraph attending the throne flew over, and touched him at the very point where he felt most unworthy. In God's hands he was to become God's mouthpiece to meet the demands of the hour. Precisely the same happens to the disciples who accompanied Jesus in response to his call in the Gospels. When the terrible deep darkness meets us, God may be in the heart of it in life-changing, awesome love, and we come through the darkness into a new clarity of light. But sometimes we are trapped in its power, with no one to help.

Deep darkness as depression

It is natural to think of images of the grave and Sheol relating to some kind of future life. No doubt they do. But to the writers of the Bible they can relate to the existential situation now. The authors of Job and the Psalms express these feelings common to the faithful, as well as the fickle and rebellious, who know the misery of depression from the inside. In such a state it is impossible to 'pull yourself together'. Sufferers commonly feel trapped and imprisoned, misunderstood and abandoned even when surrounded by sympathetic listeners, 'dead' in all but name.

The late Frank Lake, founder of the Clinical Theology movement, used to say that in depression, the best psalms to meditate on are those in multiples of eleven. From time to time I have been comforted by his good advice. Depressives take the whole guilt of the world on top of them, and if they are believers, feel particularly wretched that their faith is so impotent. They need to be encouraged to articulate their true feelings before God. He can take it. He has borne it in Jesus Christ! Psalm 88 sets a good example of honesty. It is the only one which reflects a mood of unrelieved gloom throughout, has been a great comfort to the depressed, and to all who have felt abandoned by God.

I am like those who have no help,
like those forsaken among the dead,
like the slain that lie in the grave,
like those whom you remember no more,

for they are cut off from your hand.
You have put me in the depths of the Pit,
in the regions dark and deep.
Your wrath lies heavy upon me,
and you overwhelm me with all your waves.
(Psalm 88.4–7)

What a magnificent conflation of *tehom* images! Here we have the sequence dead–grave–Pit–dark–deep–overwhelm, and waves, all in four short verses. This psalm is like a big wastebin into which we can dump all our negative feelings and experiences. So here, the writer is desperate. He feels God is hiding from him, and is beyond answering his prayers. He is overwhelmed with God's wrath. He is sleepless, crying out night and day. He is abandoned by his friends, who find him a *thing of horror*, trapped and abandoned. This experience is multifaceted, incoherent and violent. Other similar psalms add one extra dimension, the cry for vengeance on those who have put him there!

Walter Brueggemann, in his book *Praying the Psalms*, encourages us to revel in this three-dimensional poetry to the full:

> In the Psalms the use of language does not *describe* what is. It takes what has not yet been spoken, and *evokes* it into being. This kind of speech resists discipline, shuns precision, delights in ambiguity, is profoundly creative, and is in itself an exercise in freedom. In using speech in this way, we are in fact doing on a smaller scale what God has done in the Creation narratives of Genesis. We are calling into being that which does not yet exist.[7]

This, he says, is the language of surprise. It is dangerous and revolutionary because its very use constitutes a threat to all that has been up to now, including our depressed state.

In other words, here we have the language of movement in the relationship between the writer and God. Brueggemann points to two common images in the Psalms: the Pit, and the protective Wing as representing the experience of *dis*orientation (leaving one place in the journey of faith), and *re*orientation (finding one's new rightful place). The Bible is a book of journeys, and this drama is as old as the experience of Abraham and Sarah as they moved from the security of Haran to the land God would show them. And it is as vital in the journey of faith as Jesus' call to the disciples by the seashore to leave the security of their nets and their relatives and follow him. So, Brueggemann notes that 'those who stay with the image are able to speak not only in prospect of the Pit, or in the midst of trouble, but also after the trouble, in a mood of joy.'[8] So that famous beginning of Psalm 40:

I waited patiently for the Lord;
he inclined to me and heard my cry.
He drew me up from the desolate pit,
out of the miry bog,
and set my feet upon a rock,
making my steps secure.
He put a new song in my mouth,
a song of praise to our God.
Many will see and fear,
and put their trust in the Lord.

(Psalm 40.1–3)

Here, the psalm stays with the pit image right from patient waiting through rescue, to secure footholds, songs of praise and testimony to others. So the pit motif enables the speaker not only honestly to present every aspect of the miseries of life to God and have them dealt with, but also to remember afterwards what it was like to be 'in the pits', and to move on from that experience to a new celebration of life with God! So a life of faith does not protect people from darkness or 'the pits', rather it testifies to the possibility of moving beyond them to the new place where we ought to be with the God of resurrection!

Brueggemann then contrasts the pit imagery with that of the wing, which also occurs in these psalms of lament. Whereas 'pit' speaks of danger and threat, 'wing' speaks of protection and nurture. He quotes Psalm 61 to illustrate

Lead me to the rock that is higher than I;
for you are my refuge, a strong tower against the enemy.
Let me abide in your tent forever, find refuge under the shelter of your wings.

(Psalm 61.2–4)

Here is another wonderful cluster of images: rock–refuge–tower–tent–wings, words which have all the feeling of security-in-the-battle-of-life. They look forward beyond the present situation of distress, and like the 'pit' psalms they are not confined to songs of misery and despondency. While honestly facing the fact that the writer might be 'in the pits', they assert that God can be a refuge NOW. In other words they subvert and deny the legitimacy of the hold of the Pit on the worshipper's life, and transport them verbally to the Wings. So these great prayers take sufferers verbally 'from the place of powerlessness to utter safety, that is from death to life . . . To risk such prayer is to repent of the old orientation to which we no longer belong. It is to refuse to remain in the pit – which first must be fully experienced – for the sake of the wings which may be boldly anticipated.'[9]

In the 'ups and downs' of our life and faith journey, we constantly move between the Pit and the Wing. Some of us given to depression may go down much deeper than others into the mire of the deep, and feel doubly grateful that the 'wing' also includes a 'rock', bringing sure relief from the roaring waters that may suddenly flood the desert wadis in our lives. Christians will delight in New Testament parallels, which we shall examine in the light of Jesus' temptation, cross, and descent into hell.

So God's work of creation and re-creation of what is flawed is not yet finished. As parts of that created world, he has not finished with us either. At times, we still become aware of that deep, dark, chaotic water in our innermost souls. And the empty desert. And the darkness present in our consciousness, and the awesome shadows of our deep unconscious. The Pit and the Wing in the symbolism of creation represent the mighty *tehom* and the constantly brooding Spirit. Through these encounters with the grace of God and the power of the deep in our pilgrimage, little by little, personality is healed and re-created, new life transcends the old ways and we become the whole people God has designed us to be. The Spirit of God who fluttered over those dark waters at the beginning is still there now. He can create something new and beautiful through the pain of bringing new things to birth.

Chapter 5

THE CHURCH: BRIDGE OVER TROUBLED WATERS?

You have seen the house built, you have seen it adorned
By one who came in the night, it is now dedicated to God
It is now a visible church, one more light set on a hill
In a world confused and dark and disturbed by portents of fear,
And what shall we say of the future . . . ?[1]

This is a troubled world, a world which is witnessing a 'twilight of the gods'. Today, every one of the godlike powers which seemed to guarantee a sound future for the Western world view and give it a secure fabric in 1900 has been found wanting. As we enter a new millennium, huge question-marks stand over the future and status of science and technology, the free market and the global market-place, military might, the monarchy, the Church, national and local government, the nature of law and the judiciary, the family, traditional patterns of work, social values, and the very foundations of human and sexual identity.

This is also the age of anxiety, of tranquillizers and hypertension, of social, family and personal breakdown. The age, as we have seen, whose demise is foreshadowed and exemplified by the *Titanic* disaster. Today the great ship *Progress* is faltering. There are many who are still cheerfully dancing to the band in the grand ballroom on the upper deck, barely aware that the way of life and the world view they hold dear is fatally holed. But they know in their bones something is wrong, and the dark chaotic waters of the deep are threatening. Hence the passion for 'in-depth' investigative journalism, for judicial committees and royal commissions to find out what.

The woeful lack of attention given to the spiritual needs and spiritual education of Western society leaves us ill-equipped to deal with the impending sense of crisis of confidence in the whole basis of our civilization. Paul Tillich's famous and prophetic New York sermon, the *Shaking of the Foundations*, from Isaiah 24, is coming true.[2] There is a sense of foreboding as people contemplate the future in these apocalyptic times. One reaction of the Christian Church to the sense of deliverance from final judgement at the end of the first millennium was to build magnificent cathedrals in thanksgiving. If the Greenwich Dome is the best we can do to celebrate life a thousand years on, the prospects for humanity are bleak indeed.

At such a time many might be expected to look to the Church to be a haven standing for security, stable beliefs and proven values for living while the rest of society crumbles around it. In 1992 Swedish TV journalist Annika Hagström wrote her book *Like a Bridge Over Troubled Waters* with a pastor in the Kista suburb of Stockholm, about the role of the Church when a number of children died in a bus accident in his parish. It is encouraging that the ministry of the local church was perceived to be so positive among the natural and inevitable expressions of outrage and incomprehension at the time.[3] Clearly this impression was even more marked in the Swedish Church's ministry to a bereaved nation in the *Estonia* tragedy two years later, from the accounts referred to in Chapter 2. All Christians and sympathetic fellow-travellers hope for the same from the Church at a time of personal or national crisis. But many then go on to make a much more hazardous assumption. Somehow they believe their faith, expressed in prayer, worship and church membership, is a kind of investment against future pain, troubles and even life-threatening disaster. Years of faithful religious observance are supposed to build up credit against the day. God will somehow organize and rein in the winds and waves of the deep so they will soar above it, safe in the arms of mother Church, unscathed.

Such attitudes are common, but only expressed openly after tragedies happen, in the inevitable question, 'Why . . . ?' They smack more of magic than of true religion. It is hardly surprising that people enlist the help of faith to control the circumstances of life to make it as pleasurable and pain-free as possible. Such control is part of the Enlightenment myth of human invincibility, and a natural part of Western consumer expectation these days. But it presupposes a view of reality which is as old as classical Greek mythology, where there is an 'above' of delight and pleasure, which contrasts with the 'below' of present existence. And the whole purpose of life is to make sure you arrive at that blissful state in the end. If you can anticipate bliss now, so much the better. Religion can be part of the technique you use to get there in an age where technology is supreme. It might be a good alternative bet if you are always a loser in the National Lottery jackpot!

Popular dualism

The classical background for this thinking is illustrated in the *Song of Destiny*, which Johannes Brahms set to music to contrast suffering humanity's predicament with the bliss of the heavenly world:

> In the light there above, blessed spirits,
> you wander in Elysian fields!
> Shimmering celestial breezes
> touch you gently,
> as the players finger
> the sacred strings.
> Free from destiny, like a sleeping babe,
> the celestial beings breathe;
> preserved chaste
> in modest bud
> their spirit blooms
> for ever in them,
> and their blissful eyes
> shine eternally
> in still serenity.[4]

Recent centuries have assumed a strong contrast between the earthly and heavenly mode of existence, or the sacred and secular, just as much as classical thought. This way of understanding reality or dualism is illustrated in Figure 2. In this diagram, the majority of modern people sit publicly below the line in their thinking, while occasionally speculating privately about whether anything real lies above, and wondering if they ought to do something about it. The only modification sceptics might wish to make to this diagram is to put *darkness* above with *light* and *values* below. Pious believers on the other hand hope their devotion will ensure they will belong to the world above even while their feet are firmly fixed to the ground. This is especially true when worshipping in church when they can be sure the naughty sinful world lies safely locked out beyond the church door. There, heavenly bliss can be anticipated without sinful distraction! Believers and sceptics then, separate into two distinct groups with their own way of describing reality, united only by the common origin of their world views. A caricature maybe, but not by very much!

Above

future hope **GOD** and angels *then*

power of the Holy Spirit

sacred *grace* *light* *faith* *values*

heavenly soul spiritual peace and rest

---

earthly body worldly temptation and conflict

secular world of nature *darkness* *science & politics* *facts*

pull of the 'world' and the flesh

present reality **THE DEVIL** and demons *now*

Below

Figure 2 Popular dualism

It is easy to see how the holistic Hebrew biblical cosmology of Figure 1 became subtly modified to become this essentially dualistic Greek-inspired model. Most Christians reading the Bible from a New Testament perspective would not spot the difference unless it was pointed out. In the New Testament sharply opposing terms like 'light' and 'darkness' in John, and 'flesh' and 'spirit' or 'soul' and 'body' in Paul are frequently used. Such terms are commonplace in the Greek world-view of the period, and the early missionaries found them a convenient medium in which to share the gospel in the Mediterranean world. In doing so, the Christian faith they spread came dangerously close to becoming a Gnostic sect. Gnostics believed that salvation consisted in the soul being delivered through secret spiritual knowledge from a sinful body on an earth dominated by evil powers, to a lost heaven. Controversies between orthodox theologians and heresy often revolved around the theme of real or apparent dualism during the early Christian centuries. The great Christian creeds are testimony to the victory of Trinitarian faith in these battles. Although the orthodox passionately rejected thoroughgoing dualism, Christian doctrine was still expressed down the centuries in the thought forms of Plato and Aristotle rather than in Hebrew patterns of thinking. Hence Christian beliefs at a popular level about God, Jesus, sin, Satan, heaven and hell have all tended to be understood in a dualistic fashion by both Catholics and Protestants, rather than as affirming an essential unity between heaven and earth. Here is a typical example from a familiar traditional hymn:

> Pleasant are thy courts above
> In the land of light and love;
> Pleasant are thy courts below
> In this land of sin and woe:
> O, my spirit longs and faints
> For the converse of thy saints,
> For the brightness of thy face,
> For thy fullness, God of grace.[5]

Notice the number of parallels with Figure 2, and the parallels with the 'heavenly' imagery of Hölderlin's poem. Most Western people have been brought up to describe reality with a clear division between sacred and secular. It is the assumed language of folk religion. Such dualism has bedevilled the Church down the years, and inhibited its congregations in their thinking, their living and their mission. 'Keep religion out of politics!' they cry. Many Christian people refer to the world as though it was a necessary evil to be endured, rather than a place to be redeemed, where God's Spirit is forever at work. Unbelievers are to be saved *from* the world rather than *for* the world where God can use them. The devil is spoken of as though he has a free rein beyond the church door. Good believers hope and pray they'll be able to dodge him, or resist him, but feel safer singing hymns. They don't for a minute realize he might be right there with them in church all along!

Such devout people faithfully pray for families because, for some reason, home is thought a little less worldly, and anyway Jesus grew up in one. They sometimes pray for teachers and doctors, because

Jesus was seen to teach and heal, but rarely pray for one another to do a good job or be a good employer and make right decisions, forgetting that our Lord was the son of a carpenter. This is especially true for those occupations vital to the nation's health which involve politics, finance, industry and commerce and which are far too 'worldly'! They undervalue art, music and poetry unless the artist, composer or poet was known to have a Christian faith, or paints or writes on a 'Christian' theme. Evangelism and social action are polarized instead of being integrated as a united mission agenda for the Church. Even worse, dualistic thinking has contributed to shameful racist and paternalistic attitudes by white Christians against blacks, as white people ('light' coloured people) have projected the unacceptable dark traits of their own personalities onto their black neighbours. No wonder they have nothing much positive to say to the world at large, and the world thinks the Church has nothing to offer them!

So the main benefit of belonging to the Church according to this kind of thinking is to anticipate heaven here on earth by distancing the Church from the world as far as possible and being part of the 'above', and praying for the second coming soon. Here is the stuff of revivalism, holiness movements, tight church membership requirements and, taken to extremes, exclusive cults. It means that in church we ought to find a rapidly-becoming-sinless brand of like-minded people who aren't sullied with problems of sex, greed and violence. If we can find heavenly peace and union with our God away from a storm-tossed, sin-stained world, then our church fellowship really is a 'Bridge Over Troubled Waters' whatever may come of the rest of humanity down below. But does any church really measure up to that kind of expectation? And anyway who would want to join such an odd band of the life-avoiding kind of people who might make up the congregation?

Popular fundamentalism

Christian fundamentalism is a particular response of believers to the fears and uncertainties provoked by the scientific revolution of the last 150 years. It emerged in public consciousness as a reaction to Charles Darwin and the evolution controversy. Since then, we have become starkly aware of fundamentalism in all the great religions of the world. It is another way of the Church being a 'Bridge Over

Troubled Waters' for the faithful. Although the term was first used of a particular brand of nineteenth-century Protestant theology, there are plenty of conservative Catholic fundamentalists seeking to preserve traditional Roman Catholic teaching in matters like women priests, abortion and birth control. Literal beliefs in the infallibility of holy church or holy book are attractive for those who are looking for a solid framework and structure for faith amid modern confusion and controversies of faith. They bring a sense of certainty and reassurance, right teaching and the victory of God (in their favour of course) while the rest of the world goes down the tube. In this way, fundamentalism has links with popular dualism. It is easy to lampoon them, but they are a large, diverse and anxious bunch of heartfelt believers who deserve to be listened to rather than constantly vilified by those who do not share their opinions. They are also growing in numbers, at a time when everyone appears to be all at sea in beliefs and moral values.

Fundamentalists are true sons and daughters of the Enlightenment. They have taken science to heart and do all they can to make the faith as reasonable as possible. That doesn't mean that faith shouldn't involve the proper use of our minds. It just means that they go overboard on 'proving' everything literally from the Bible, riding roughshod over poetry, metaphor, mystery and symbol in order to do so. Doubts are basically bad for believers and are sent by Satan to undermine faith. Perhaps it would be truer to say that doubts undermine superficial religious 'certainties', which is not quite the same thing. It never occurs to them to see that doubting 'certainties' might be a healthy way for faith to grow to maturity. That is after all how children learn to grow up to face life as healthy adults.

Fundamentalists also tend to see the Bible as a flat surface, of equal inspiration for all people at all times, making no apparent distinction in value between the laws of sacrifice in Leviticus (which may indeed have been God's inspired word for the people of Israel at the time) and the teaching of Jesus Christ in the Gospels. In order to do this, they have to use allegory and typology to interpret obscure passages, despite their express belief in the literal truth of holy Scripture. In other words, having emptied Scripture of symbol and mystery by literalizing its meaning, they then have to re-mystify it in order to put their own special spin on particular passages. This is tantamount to a new kind of Gnosticism, where particular preachers are followed for their insights into the hidden depths of the Bible, to impart to the faithful deep knowledge which will help them to escape the temptations of the wicked world before it is too late. Anyone who has suffered a long sermon on the identity of the 'Beast' in Revelation will take the point! Sometimes ingenious Bible expositors have led whole generations of clergy down obscure backwaters of scriptural exegesis. Charles Schofield's *Annotated Bible* sold over two million copies at its first printing when published in America in 1915. His ingenious notes with their wholly artificial notion of 'Dispensations' of God in Scripture are still influencing millennial aspirations among some devout believers on both sides of the Atlantic today.

Loss of faith and disillusionment with the Church

In a world suffering from disaster overload, it is inevitably awash with people who are angry, disappointed and disillusioned with the Church and God when what they had hoped for doesn't happen or isn't apparently true. They hoped that being part of the Church would somehow insulate them from the roaring of the depths, whether unforeseen catastrophes or daily pressures. That particular techniques of prayer or worship would bring promised miraculous healing to their bodies and souls. That the Lord would have come again by now in particular visible ways, as Scripture promises (according to certain preachers), and it hasn't happened; that much-vaunted divine 'proofs' and 'certainties' proclaimed by particular branches of the Church are actually shot through with holes. But then not even the Church, it appears to some, is sure what it believes about God any more; many outside its fellowship have apparently ceased to bother. The secure 'Bridge Over Troubled Waters' many once trusted has collapsed into the sea of chaos and confusion. They feel betrayed by the Church, they are deeply hurt and often openly claim to have lost their faith. They have joined the great army of moderns who view the land above the sacred/secular divide with scepticism. They view the minority who are still church members as hypocrites or antiquarian oddities; or misguided worshippers of an illusion.

Inevitably religion is blamed for many of the world's ills. No one can deny that many of the most bitter conflicts in the world today have religious components to them. The enmity between Arab and Jew in the Middle East is as old as Esau and Jacob, and that between Christianity and Islam as old as the crusades. The three-way conflict between Croats, Serbs and Balkan Muslims dates from the fourteenth century; the hostility between Catholics and Protestants in Northern Ireland, indelibly marked by the Battle of the Boyne in 1690, is still celebrated in marching and aggressive posturing. Add to that inter-religious battles between Sikhs, Hindus and Muslims in India; and between Christians and Muslims in Cyprus, Sudan, Nigeria and the Philippines; the appalling legacy of the Dutch Reformed Church's apartheid theology in South Africa; and millennarian suicide cults like the Aum Shinrikyo group in Japan; and the list looks damning.

Under the banner of public education in a free society, schools, aided and abetted by opinion-formers in the media, have hoped that by ignoring issues of, faith, religion and morality a new generation of 'men and women come of age' would be born to assist in the next stage of the world's progress towards a society free from illusion and superstition! After all, what was the point educating a new generation in such a dangerous and life-denying subject, especially if it perpetuated superstition and violence? Now science had finally banished heaven, from its medieval place above the clouds to a position beyond the farthest galaxy in a rapidly expanding universe, it could effectively be discounted! So theology departments in universities were run down, RE lessons in schools downgraded and marginalized, and good Christian teachers accused of indoctrinating their pupils if they taught with any degree of passion for the subject at all. In the West we have suffered a generation of sceptical engineering by stealth.

The legacy of true faith – and the consequences of neglect

It is natural for those who have lost faith, and who feel betrayed and abused by the religion they have known, to feel bitter and dismissive, and to want to save the next generation from similar hurt. Such people have dominated the media, and social and educational theory for a generation. But they overplay their hand. They are too dismissive, and too easily forget the benefits of the Christian faith to the whole world. The Church may be flawed; but it is not fatally compromised. The Millennium celebrations have given Christian people an opportunity to focus the attention of those outside the

Church on a common heritage. For fourteen centuries in Britain alone Christianity has been the foundation for the social, legal, educational and political fabric of our lives. The Christian faith has been a spur to a vast range of human advances in civilization, adventure, courage, compassion and healing. The Christian story has inspired much of the greatest music, art, literature and poetry. Many of the finest and most influential scientists have actually been Christians and many are today. Above all, being a disciple of Jesus Christ has changed the lives of millions for the better, giving them coherence and hope.

With the dawn of a new millennium, the legacy of neglect is all too apparent. Breakdown of the moral consensus and social cohesion is rife. People have lost the link with that great story which has united them hitherto in a common interdependence and purpose. David Hay comments,

> The adult world into which our children are inducted is more often than not destructive to their spirituality. I am not thinking simply of an inventory of the human woes that people wring their hands about. I have in mind something that underlies this, the process that goes on in the consciousness of children as they assimilate popular culture.[6]

Media images and Virtual Reality provide new mythology for empty souls which is little more permanent than the Top Ten Video Chart.

Pressure from other faiths far less accommodating than Christians to Western secularizing tendencies is prompting a new search for core values which is even finding its way onto the political agenda. From 1997 RE is once more part of the core curriculum in English schools. Per Pettersson reports that a year after the *Estonia* disaster, religious education was once more restored as a compulsory subject in the Swedish high school curriculum.[7] Theology departments in universities are full. Many of the greatest questions being asked today are faith-related. The media are suddenly coming alive with faith and life issues. Heaven won't go away. It may still be very near after all. Many people are searching for faith again, but they are severely handicapped. Two generations of scepticism have deprived them of a language through which they can explore spiritual realities with integrity, and sing the Lord's song without lapsing into Victorian clichés.

The Church, and by implication God himself, appears a great

disappointment to many modern people because the model of reality on offer to successive generations has been false. The divide between sacred and secular is a completely artificial construct, and Christian believers have connived with modern sceptics by perpetuating it. While heaven and earth remain, church members cannot distance themselves from the murky waters of the deep any more than anyone else. As we saw in the last chapter, every believer embodies the deep *within* themselves. Faith in itself cannot magic the deep away because Christian people are part of the problem! The collective unconscious of any religious institution can represent the ambigious power of the deep at its worst as well as shine the love of God at its best. While the Church is a haven for storm-tossed travellers, and is an important bridge between God and humanity, it is also fallen like the rest of the cosmos. Yet God is at work there and by his grace the Church can still be a true advertisement for human transformation and a renewed society. And the Church can still point to where the creative wind of the Spirit is at work on the face of the waters within the world. That is where the powers of the deep are still being confronted, tamed and directed in God's mysterious economy. That is where renewed creation is being born and where shocks and labour pains are still being felt. That is where the Word bridged the sacred/secular divide and became flesh! The future is with God in a *new earth* as well as a new heaven (Revelation 21.1).

Kosmos *and the* Kosmokratores

This point becomes clearer when we consider carefully what the New Testament means by 'the world', so that it is always thought of as the place where God is at work, and not the exclusive preserve of the devil. The Greek word *kosmos* means most of what we might expect of the word 'world' in English, like the created order, the planet earth, and the theatre of human life. But in places in the New Testament, particularly in John's Gospel, *kosmos* has a special meaning. Walter Wink shows how, for example when Jesus is speaking to the high priest at his trial, 'I have spoken openly to the world [*kosmos*]; I have always taught in synagogues and in the temple' (John 18.20).

The parallelism in this sentence indicates that here, *kosmos* includes at least the central religious institutions of Judaism, where Jesus

> has declared his message. The term thus has a structural sense. It refers, in this instance, to a religious system that, as the author portrays it, is unaware of its alienation from God.

Wink helpfully coins the phrase 'Domination System' for *kosmos*, to include all the spiritual, social, political and personal powers alienated from God. This brings a whole new understanding to familiar Johannine phrases like 'I am not of this world' (John 8.23), which seems to imply the dualistic notion that Jesus is not really human at all, and that the created order is essentially evil. What Jesus is saying to the Pharisees is simply, 'You belong to the world Domination System. I belong to God's system.'[8]

The Domination System tells people what is 'politically correct' and what isn't. The media and public opinion are its handmaids, and they are as fickle as current fashion. It tells us what to *believe*. Today, for example, it is 'PC' to have personal religious beliefs, provided they don't affect anyone else, but regular church membership is a waste of time. It tells us what to *value*, like wealth and consumption, the myth of conquest through violence, and everything in the TV advertisements. It tells us what to *see*, filling our vision with the material, and calling the spiritual illusion. What a contrast with Jesus Christ, who offers the world – with its many rival systems of political, social, economic and religious power mixing good and evil – a new reality called the Kingdom, which means new faith, new values, and new vision! Ephesians goes one stage further:

> ... our struggle is not against enemies of blood and flesh, but against the rulers, against the authorities, against the cosmic powers of this present darkness, against the spiritual forces of evil in the heavenly places.
>
> (Ephesians 6.12)

The oppressive *kosmos* of John's writing is now split into a whole range of forces under the general heading of *cosmic powers* with the same Greek root (*kosmokratores*). Many commentators think this passage just speaks about the invisible demonic. This cannot be. We have just seen how religion and its laws are part of the Domination System which crucified Jesus Christ, and continues to oppose God's purposes. Spiritual powers always have their physical equivalents: all that is oppressive and life-denying, including religious beliefs, traditions and rituals; all that would keep people apart in family life, education, social status, racial and sexual discrimination; all institutional idolatry, political rhetoric, oppressive economic theory and practice. Any one of these can exhibit demonic power. In Revelation 13 the link between the cosmic powers and the deep is quite explicit. The prophet John, touched by the spirit of God 'sees' a reality which is invisible to others – that all-too-familiar monster of idolatrous political power and plausible propaganda enshrined within it, rising up out of the symbolic *tehom*. This monster used to come up literally out of the sea, with the arrival of the Roman proconsul at Ephesus.

The Domination System can be redeemed

Of course it would be quite wrong to represent institutions like the family, the police and judiciary, government agencies, financial and industrial institutions and social services as totally evil. They are not. They were created good: God knows how much they are necessary to provide values, cohesion and mutual care and worthwhile purpose for all societies. But in the world that God is creating *heaven* and *earth* must be under Christ, his ways, his purposes, his authority. These powers are not immortal, they are not gods, and they are not designed to operate independently from the one true God. Like 'Adam' and 'Eve' they are fallen creatures. As they go astray, they take on an independent life of their own. They become idolatrous, taking on a sinister autonomy offering a 'salvation' of their own. Then they become oppressors of those who do not think and act their way. The methods of the old-fashioned Soviet state in Estonia and modern millennial cults are not so very different. They are part of the dark, restless, rebellious deep. So the Domination System, which groups together a whole host of sub-systems, designed to bring cohesion to life, actually becomes life-destructive. But this System of powers can be redeemed, like everything else in all creation. The deep can be reclaimed. The Spirit of God is still brooding lovingly over the waters, patiently working, moulding, remoulding the chaotic dark maelstrom of the unreconciled cosmos.

> God did not send the Son into the created universe [*kosmos*] to condemn the System [*kosmos*], but that the System [*kosmos*] might be saved through him.
>
> (John 3.17, adapted from NRSV)

Where does this leave the Church then? Not, as we have seen, *above* the waters of the deep, because we are not in the business of preaching a gospel of salvation *from* the messy and murky world, but the transformation of heaven and earth now, as a foretaste of what is to come. Sometimes the Church can be part of the very essence of the hostile waters. This always happens when church denominations and fellowships become exclusive, suffocating and life-denying, under the guise of biblical teaching, evangelical shibboleths, liberal assumptions, Catholic practice, or anything else that legitimizes them in the eyes of their members. By doing this they can so easily embody an oppressive and idolatrous spirituality, hostile to God's ways, working against the loving and express will of Christ.

If we are to be any use at all to the hurt, the faithless and the disillusioned, the Church must reject all temptations to be otherworldly or exclusive. We must be there with them *on* the waters, living with the constant threat of the power of the wind and the waves of the deep, where the Spirit of Jesus Christ is at work. Our invitation to them is, 'Hear the voice and take the hand of Jesus.' Peter is our exemplar, in the story of his walking on the water of the Sea of Galilee (Matthew 14.22–33).

This account is set in the fading light of evening, representing the present condition of the world we know, shared by faithful and faithless alike. The storm-battered boatful of disciples represents the fearful Church, which doesn't expect Jesus to be on the dark sea, and doesn't recognize him when he appears in the gloom beyond their own boat! The ever-present possibility of sinking that Peter faced once he got out of the boat and took his eyes off Jesus will keep us humble, not triumphalist, forgiving and willing to ask for forgiveness, not arrogant in our approach to those who find it difficult to believe. The assuring voice and ever-present saving hand of Jesus in the darkness will be there for our little faith as well as theirs. Whatever its failings and lack of faith, Jesus still believes in the Church. He can lead all those battered by the storms of life back to the fellowship of the boat whether they are church members or not. In the boat again they can know he is with them and find joy in his presence.

Chapter 6

MONSTERS OF THE DEEP

These yelling monsters that with ceaseless cry
Surround me, as thou sawest, hourly conceived
And hourly born, with sorrow infinite, To me . . .[1]

In Iris Murdoch's novel *The Sea, the Sea*, Charles, the central character, is trying to make a new life for himself in retirement by the sea, after a lifetime in the theatre. Soon after he arrives at his new home, he 'sees' a sea-monster a short distance from the shore, rising from the waves, and wonders what it all can mean. Shortly after, he discovers that a woman who had been an unrequited love of his life as a teenager at school has come to live a short distance away, with her husband. The book explores the way obsessive passion for her rises up within him, and how he tries to possess her and break up her marriage, until he realizes, through a near-drowning accident and the death of her son Titus, how the monster has very nearly destroyed him, and sees the error of his ways.[2]

Iris Murdoch shows in a dramatic way how the dark, chaotic, empty primal *tehom* can take on personality. Sometimes that personality is derived from the way movements of the deep are perceived in the circumstances of life and in the human heart as in Charles's case. In the Bible too the deep has personality. Psalm 93 speaks of the voice of the flood sounding with its winds and waves, while Psalm 98 tells of the clapping of the waves at the prospect of the Lord coming in judgement. At other times, the deep takes its personality from the monsters which swim within it like the legendary Rahab or Leviathan, alias the dragon, a hangover from the mythic Babylonian Tiamat. These monsters become 'visible' when they rise from their natural habitat to take concrete form in the dehumanized cosmic powers that arrogantly oppose God and the establishment of true human values.

I, Daniel, saw in my vision by night the four winds of heaven

> stirring up the great sea, and four great beasts came up out of the sea, different from one another.
>
> (Daniel 7.2–3)

Such oppressive spiritual forces are equally well represented in material and political terms by powerful political, economic and military forces whose influence is represented by the deserts of steel and concrete skyscrapers rising from the heart of big cities as well as by armies and navies! Or by the twists and turns of all that is buried in the human heart. Here is an important clue to understanding the best-known monster of the deep, Satan himself, and the demons, his accomplices.

The spiritual within the material

The thought that the spiritual can reside in the material may seem strange to those used to thinking in the dualistic way already explored. Yet it is as old as Genesis 1, the Psalms, the 'Word made flesh', and the institution of the Eucharist, Celtic spirituality, the life of St Francis of Assisi, the poetry of William Wordsworth, and the thought of Archbishop William Temple, who delighted in shocking congregations by referring to Christianity as the most materialistic of world religions. All spiritual reality created by God has to be 'embodied' and expressed through people and things.

This is not a plea for New Age pantheism by the back door. God is not *the same* as the created world of heaven and earth. He is 'above the heavens'. Jesus Christ 'passed through the heavens' (Hebrews 4.14), yet he upholds, inhabits and sustains the whole created cosmos by his Spirit. It is simply another way to express the sacramental principle at the heart of all life, from sub-atomic particles to remote galaxies. The Bible is delightfully imprecise about this spiritual world, so that 'spirits', 'principalities and powers', 'rulers' and 'authorities', 'angels' and 'demons' inhabit very *concrete* phenomena, structures and institutions and people.

Amazingly, this is the way most people *talk* about life and their own feelings whether they claim to have faith or not! Unsophisticated everyday language is remarkably accurate in the way it describes the spirituality of the world. It is quite natural for 'non-religious' people to speak of the spirit of their football team or the Internet.

Male and female representations of the 'spirits' of the weather introduce ITV forecasts each night after the main news bulletins. Nations and tribal groups, corporate companies, football teams, the City, trade unions, the media, churches, young and old, rich and poor all have spirits of one kind or another, which can be depressed, or elated. Spin-doctors, promotional advertisements and image consultants are all about changing the inner spirit or perception people have of governments as well as commercial products. Spirituality in the material is represented in a different way by Antony Gormley's 200-ton *Angel of the North* statue just outside Gateshead on the A1, erected in 1998, with a wing-span of a jumbo jet. This copper and steel representation of the resilient strength of the people of the region is one of the most striking examples of modern public art.

Spirits are found in liquid material form in every bar and off-licence – they can excite, depress, and otherwise affect the outward behaviour of those who drink them. Alcoholism is literally a spiritual problem, 'demon drink', as Alcoholics Anonymous recognizes only too clearly. The first disciples appeared to onlookers to have been drinking on the day of Pentecost. From this angle there should be no difficulty recognizing at least some of the claimed *physical* manifestations and benefits of the Toronto Blessing, experienced in charismatic churches recently, as genuine evidence of the indwelling Holy Spirit.

The Bible confirms popular expressions of the spiritual within the material in other ways. In the apocalypse of Daniel, for example, each nation has its own 'angel' (Daniel 10–12). The recent history of Estonia suggests that its own national spirit or angel has been more sympathetic to a Christian outlook, successfully resisting the alien philosophy of Marxism for fifty years. Revelation mentions another group of spirits, the angels of the seven churches of Asia Minor, which express the corporate personality of their respective fellowships:

> And to the angel of the church in Laodicea write: The words of the Amen, the faithful and true witness, the origin of God's creation: . . . Let anyone who has an ear listen to what the Spirit is saying to the churches.
>
> (Revelation 3.14, 22)

These instances show how the Spirit of God can work powerfully at the same level of human personality as other spirits, whether conscious, subconscious or unconscious, individual or corporate. Carl Jung spoke of this inner spiritual dimension to life as the collective unconscious, an amazing network of spiritual vitality inhabiting everyone and everything. It is within this network that God is constantly at work, and Satan and the demonic is revealed as well. It is from this perspective that we can speak with clarity to the issue of 'demonic possession'. The truth is we are in fact all 'possessed'! The spirits that possess our being will determine our outlook and behaviour, 'whose we are and whom we serve'.

Lord of the darkness

In the Bible, God is responsible in the end for everything, for good and even for ill, a viewpoint passionately held by orthodox Jews to this day, but not always by Christians. This uncomfortable truth is easily forgotten

> I am the Lord, and there is no other.
> I form light and create darkness,
> I make weal and create woe;
> I the Lord do all these things.
>
> (Isaiah 45.6–7)

It is verses like these that establish a link between the outlook of Second Isaiah (chapters 40–55) and the first chapter of Genesis. In Genesis, the connection between God and woe is more opaque. Darkness was part of the chaotic 'non-being' of the *tehom* that became something good through the action of the Spirit of God. Darkness has the right to exist for now under God's control, along with the monsters of the deep who fill the created waters in the world of Genesis 1 and Psalm 104. In the Bible, God is seen to be firmly in control of the advance and retreat of the flood both in judgement and salvation, whether in floods of water, or floods of enemy soldiers as the monsters rear their heads and flay their tails. Satan and his minions represent the ultimate development of the 'personality' of the Bible's sea monsters, the interior spiritual personality of the *tehom*, which can all too easily be 'felt' in physical and material sense experience.

Where does Satan come from? Walter Wink has provided the most perceptive treatment I know, in his book *Unmasking the Powers*,[3] which has inspired my own thinking below. Jewish and Christian understanding of Satan grew, like the theology of the deep, from hard experience. It was Abraham, before the destruction of Sodom, who first posed the question millions of puzzled and outraged believers and unbelievers want to pose to God in their passion for justice:

> Shall not the Judge of all the earth do what is just?
>
> (Genesis 18.25)

Satan as God's agent who puts people to the test

The Hebrew word *satan* means 'adversary'. Surprisingly it does not receive a mention in the parable of the Fall. It is used of enemies of Israel in 1 Samuel 29 and 1 Kings 5 and 11. In the latter cases they are raised up by the Lord rather like the action of the flood on other occasions. The angel who bars the way of Balaam's ass on God's orders in Numbers 22 is called '*his satan*'. Satan appears in only three other places in the Old Testament, and always as God's agent. Satan receives his most thorough Old Testament exposure in the book of Job, where he is a proper name worthy of a capital letter for the first time. The book of Job is conceived as a brilliant and merciless jibe at the rich who are popularly perceived to enjoy their money and status because of God's blessing. The prophets complain time and time again when rich people use their privileged status to oppress the poor, adding insult to the injury that God might view them as second-class citizens anyway.

In the story of Job the writer poses the hypothetical question 'What if an extremely rich and godly man were to . . . ?' and interpolates it into an ancient folk-tale. Satan is God's go-between, and a member of the heavenly court in the drama. He never has any power other than that God gives him. He is there to ask awkward questions and sift motives. Satan shows himself magnificently on the side of the dispossessed and downtrodden, exactly representing their views in their worst moments of humiliation at the hands of the wealthy! In a strange way, the book of Job is an answer to those passionate but disturbing pleas for vengeance in the Psalms. In the book, God is purged from any unjustified assumptions that the rich might have that their wealth is linked with divine favour. And humanity is given an almost unparalleled exploration of the mystery of suffering to treasure and learn from. In the Old Testament, then, Satan is clearly in the service and under the control of God.

There are a number of places in the New Testament too where Satan has this God-given role of sifter of motives, including that incident at the last supper where Jesus says to Simon Peter

> Simon, Simon, listen! Satan has demanded to sift all of you like wheat, but I have prayed for you that your own faith may not fail; and you, when once you have turned back, strengthen your brothers.
>
> (Luke 22.31–2)

Satan's job here is to test and purify the disciples' commitment. Peter was not fully aware of his inner weakness, otherwise he would never have been so impulsive. Satan's job is to make him aware of this truth, something Jesus in his ministry had been unable to do at that stage in Peter's spiritual journey. Jesus promises his prayers in the test – not that he will be excused the trial! This illustrates well what is meant by Satan's capacity to 'tempt'. The word translated temptation (*peirasmos*) means 'test', or 'trial' involving considerable effort. Hence the advice of James,

> Submit yourselves therefore to God. Resist the devil, and he will flee from you.
>
> (James 4.7)

Precisely, Satan has no power unless we give it to him. When I took my first steps in faith following Jesus Christ, I remember soon after questioning my decision and my motives, and have experienced inner struggles in thought and prayer on many occasions since. I *needed* Satan to test me, and show me the step I had taken was genuine and right. When I found the courage to resist this inner voice, I found out that God was more real to me than before. In the outcome of these tussles, with the help and prayers of friends, I gradually found the strength to continue my pilgrimage. Countless disciples have begun to discover their new identity as Christians through the same process.

Jesus' 'temptation'

After his baptism, and before beginning his public ministry, Jesus has to discover his role as Messiah-king. The Spirit drives him out into the Judaean desert for forty days and nights, and Satan is sent to him to enable him to discover it. He does so by presenting him with Jewish Messianic expectations in the form of three questions. First, to prove his Sonship by a wilderness manna miracle, like Moses. But he has already heard at his baptism that he is Son, and God will provide, so he refuses. Second, to prove himself an invulnerable superhuman being by taking part in a dramatic suicidal act in the Temple (not unlike a modern *Superman* or *Batman* stunt). He will not do that, even if Satan quotes Scripture to egg him on. Third, to embrace kingly power like David, in the form of world empire; and Jesus will have none of it.

What is happening here? The Jews were looking for a prophet like Moses, a priestly Messiah, and a Davidic king. They knew exactly what they were expecting – it is in all the intertestamental literature, writ large. Scripture even pointed that way! But God's word is in none of these. Over 800 years before, Elijah found God's word not in the expected wind, earthquake and fire in the wilderness, but *in sheer silence* (1 Kings 9.11–13). Now, thanks to Satan, Jesus discovers God's word not in Jewish Messianic expectations either, *even if they are attested in Scripture!* 'Satan throws up to Jesus the collective Messianic hopes, and by so doing brings them for the first time to consciousness as options to be chosen rather than as a fate to be accepted. Tested against his own sense of calling, they did not fit. Jesus could then perceive them as "yesterday's will of God" not what was proceeding out of the mouth of God.'[4] These temptations will remain with him as he faces ever greater pressure to conform to the out-of-date concept of Messiahship demanded by public opinion. Satan will come to him later as his closest friend and disciple, Peter. When Peter recognizes Jesus as the Messiah, he immediately tries to force him into the same mould that Jesus rejected earlier in the desert wilderness! (Mark 8.31–3).

Satan acted as 'adversary' or tester of Jesus' thoughts and motives under the express will of God. As Jesus waged the battle, he discovered his true identity. This surely is why he was led by the Spirit into the wilderness. Through this painful process a 'new creation' takes place. Jesus discovers a new kind of Messiahship which is to mark the whole of his ministry: kingship through humble courageous service and sacrifice. The desert proves to be a *habitation for dragons* (cf. Isaiah 34.13 AV). But as an element of the great *tehom* under the powerful wind of the Spirit, it proves once more to be the place of revelation of God's will. The agony of the wilderness represents not just the awful physical, mental and spiritual privations. It represents the pain of choosing God's new way against the weight of people's expectations under the circumstances.

Satan as the devil

What has become of Satan as the wicked archfiend, the fallen super-power of *Paradise Lost* whose canny strength seems to rival the power of God for our wills and affections? Nothing written above explains him away or softens his image. He is very much alive and kicking, strongly represented in the intertestamental literature, the New Testament and human experience. In the New Testament, he is known as 'the devil' (i.e. the *false* tester or accuser), 'the evil one', 'the ruler of this world', 'the enemy', 'the prince of the power of the air' and so on. He goes under a veritable galaxy of names, some of which suggest links with monsters in the deep like 'the great dragon', or 'ancient serpent'. This malevolent fiend tries to frustrate God's creative purposes at every turn, binding and blinding us from experiencing and seeing the truth about him; in turn visiting disease, division and destruction on people and communities, promoting lies and unbelief. He is represented as presiding over everything that is anti-God, he meets his match in the confrontation between Jesus and the demon-possessed, and in Jesus' conflict with political and religious power which led to the cross. He will receive his come-uppance in the end, in that ultimate image of the deep, the 'lake of unquenchable fire'.

Who or what?

What kind of being is this? It would be wrong to deduce from this that Satan is a person, although he is 'personal'. Satan as the devil is experienced as an accusing and lying inner 'voice', as an almost physical force for evil, or as the collective unconscious or corporate evil spirit of gangs, institutions, systems and nations bent on life-destructive conquest and domination. He is the darkest of all the dark angels of the universe. Walter Wink describes Satan as 'a suprapersonal, non physical, spiritual agency, the collective shadow, the sum total of all the individual darkness, evil, unredeemed anger, and fear of the whole race, and all the echoes and reverberations still vibrating down through time from those who have chosen evil before us'.[5] That is a pretty comprehensive summary of cosmic fallenness. Satan as the devil makes us tend towards evil often long before we are ever aware that we are in the wrong.

And we are fallen too, not because of some kind of crude genetic transmission of sin which has led some believers to consider sex as inherently sinful; but because we are born into a society whose atmosphere and institutions are often patterned to think, to choose and to run themselves that way, and we grow up to collude with public opinion. The deepest part of the deep ocean is totally black, without light. So generation after generation as it listens to Satan, rather than resisting him, contributes actively to a deposit of unreconstructed malevolent sludge of 'non-being' in the *tehom* of the cosmos, which in the mystery of evil appears to have a momentum all its own.

And this is not by any means just a hidden presence. The variety of names given to Satan in the New Testament show how very difficult it is to pin him down. Fallen angel he may be, but he can appear as *an angel of light* (2 Corinthians 11.14). Of course he can, because he is properly experienced as ambivalent, and he takes that ambivalent role with those who are willing to go his way. One moment he is a licentious layabout. The next he is a legalistic prude. Religion, politics, personal and social morality and fantasy are all media in which he regularly operates. No wonder he is fascinating to a society starved of mystery and spirituality! Too often, however, credulous Christians and others concentrate on the lurid details of individual 'possession', and fail to appreciate how the whole world-order is infected by Satanic cancer. That lack of balance too is devilish.

Reconciling the two pictures of Satan

It is essential we are ambiguous about Satan's activities, because if we think of his activities as totally evil and anti-God we will tend to paranoia, as many Christians do! We shall use his perceived activities as an excuse for not growing up. We shall also be in danger of excusing evil when we consider it is in a 'just' cause. How then can these two functions, of Satan as God's testing agent, and Satan as the false accuser, be reconciled without lapsing into typical popular Christian dualism again? The answer seems to lie in the choices human beings make, and that takes us back to Genesis and the parable of the Fall again. The man and his wife were told

> You may freely eat of every tree of the garden; but of the tree of the knowledge of good and evil you shall not eat, for in the day that you eat of it you shall die.
>
> (Genesis 2.16–17)

In choosing to eat of the tree of the knowledge of good and evil at the invitation of the serpent, itself an ancient symbol of good (healing) as well as evil, these representatives of humanity reckoned they knew better than God. Putting a fence round this knowledge was in fact an act of grace, not the legalism of a divine spoil-sport. God tried to protect human beings from the awful dark *tehom* lying behind the light. Now that loving plan was undone, human beings in a mysterious way unravelled God's beautiful creative process. They became aware of the same primal material God had at his disposal at the beginning. Their understanding was 'darkened' (Ephesians 4.18). They could now be 'like God'. 'Knowing good and evil' does not mean, as many assume, merely a detached kind of intellectual knowledge. 'It means participation in them existentially; it means, in Hebrew, to be *able* to do what you want to do,'[6] and that brings terrifying responsibility.

We can represent the human dilemma like this.[7]

GOOD *or* EVIL

←――――――――――――――――→

Experiencing Satan as God's agent of testing	*our choices*	Colluding with Satan as the the devil

To have the freedom to choose is part of our human potential. Whether we serve the cause of humanity depends on how we choose. Satan brings to our consciousness all the options for choice, including those we conveniently forget or subconsciously bury, like, 'What will people think if . . . ?' and worse. If we choose God's way we participate in God's creative goodness. Satan will be experienced as his agent, because paradoxically we have 'resisted' him. If we think we know better than God, we consciously or unconsciously serve the cause of Satan, and contribute to that part of the world's psyche which is oppressive, idolatrous, and at its roots Satanic. The problem is that some of the choices before humanity are 'devilishly' difficult.

Much that is devilish can appear like God's will, particularly if it relates to biblical themes like law, family life, social attitudes and evangelism. The Jewish scribes illustrated this paradox in the judgement they made on Jesus' ministry. They considered Jesus infested by Beelzebul, the prince of devils, because they couldn't see that forgiving prostitutes, eating with tax-gatherers and healing on the Sabbath was part of God's new order! Jesus' wilderness temptations teach us one thing above all. Discovering God's will doesn't always come without a great deal of internal struggle in desert conditions, when we may feel most 'barren' of God's presence. And guidance is never easy when Satan can use the Bible as well. But we can be aware of the Spirit of God near us too, most of all when we are stripped of false pretensions!

Satan's minions

There is enormous current interest in the subject of the demonic. This is not the place to explore demonology in detail, or to consider appropriate ways of ministering and bringing healing to the demonized and oppressed. Our task is to relate these spiritual realities to the theme of the biblical mythology of the deep. First, what we cannot do is ascribe rational organization to the strategy and tactics of Satan and his minions, as some charismatic Christians are prone to do. Evil is not logical or rational. There is no sense to it at all. It emanates from the chaos of the *tehom*. It is God who produces beauty and order out of that. Satan is divisive, irrational and destructive, the very opposite of harmony and integration. And deceptive too. There is even a demonic kind of order, well known in the control imposed by totalitarian regimes or religious cults on their followers. The trains always run on time in fascist states, as they were reputed to do in Mussolini's Italy.

Second, there is often a strong link between the social and personal demonic, illustrated by the account of the Gerasene demoniac (Mark 5.1–20 and parallels). At this point in the gospel story Jesus has just arrived on the shore of gentile territory, the area of the Decapolis, or ten towns, having fought a battle with the *tehom*, represented by a life-threatening storm on the Sea of Galilee. The Gospel writers intend us to make a connection between the outer chaos of the natural world which often seems positively demonic in its irrational cruelty, and the inner chaos of depths of the human unconscious which threaten the stability of personal consciousness.

The ten towns had a chequered history. They were developed from the time of Alexander the Great three centuries before as city-states promoting Greek culture and religion in an area that now technically belonged to King Herod. They had gradually lost their autonomy with the demise of Greek oversight, and Gadara had subsequently suffered harsh Jewish and Roman occupation. At the time Jesus arrived, the people were required to pay taxes to Rome, and were subject to Roman military conscription. In the fateful Jewish War, they would be a base for Emperor Vespasian's legions. They felt Greek, yet were occupied and oppressed successively by Jews and Romans, and powerless to do anything about it.

There are all sorts of mysteries surrounding this story. Where was Gerasa? The real town was 30 miles from the shore of the lake, Gadara is 5 miles inland. Perhaps the best solution is to see the place as a play on words. Gadara becomes 'the driving-out place', because *garash* in Hebrew means 'to drive out'. Where is the cliff? There are no cliffs by the shore here. We sometimes speak of stories as 'cliffhangers'. Certainly when the pigs careered over the edge, the doom of the demons was decisively sealed. And what about the man in the tombs? Since it is possible to find chains to bind even possessed men with superhuman strength, how is it he managed to live? Who was feeding him or even letting him loose on occasions? Luke's account suggests he became mad on certain occasions only (Luke 8.29).

This remarkable Gospel picture is full of insight into many human conditions. The depressed know what it is to live in the tombs: that terrible experience of deadness and self-blame, which cuts them off from other people. The jealous and resentful know what it is to be eaten up with bitterness. The unforgiving and the unforgiven know only too well how they can be attracted to and repelled by Jesus Christ at the same time. All this is true, but does not account for all the details. René Girard has argued that because human societies cannot face their own inner violence, they have to devise scapegoats to act as lightning conductors. He sees the man of the tombs as a community scapegoat.[8] The local people enjoy the sight of the demonized man representing their own violence, and let him free from time to time to act out their feelings by proxy. Paradoxically he is the only free man in the community, as he pays no taxes and is not subject to conscription. He bears their repressed violence and expresses it in his self-mutilation.

Wink identifies the violence which makes him behave this way as the corporate spirit of the Roman occupying army, the 'Legion'. Like the local populace, the demonized man is an 'occupied person'.[9] He could be right. When Jesus expels the Legion, the pigs act like a Roman force on a suicide mission, back to the deep where they belong, but a deep which is still located within the territory of the community because the demons still insist they belong to the region. No wonder the people wanted Jesus to leave after their scapegoat had been healed. Their own corporate sickness can now no longer be concealed! Jesus' kingdom is always a threat to a sick society. This community has no need of a doctor, as Jesus comments elsewhere. They, like many modern dysfunctional examples, prefer to remain sick.

Slaying the monsters

The book of Revelation is a brilliant visionary 'theme and variations' on the subject of the End of all things. Like the beginning of Genesis it defies strict chronology. It is heavy with myth and symbol and full of deep poetic truth which no 'facts' can ever do justice to. At the climax, following the great final battle, the devil is thrown into the lake of fire and sulphur, together with his other cronies, the beast and the false prophet, to be tormented day and night for ever (Revelation 20.10). The sea is now not just a dark dump for sin and demonized pigs, but burns red with the fiery judgement of God, mixed with oxygen-denying sulphur to extinguish life.

This is the second attempt of the prophet John to describe the devil's demise. The first comes earlier in the chapter where we read:

> Then I saw an angel, coming down from heaven, holding in his hand the key to the bottomless pit and a great chain. He seized the dragon, that ancient serpent, who is the Devil and Satan, and bound him for a thousand years, and threw him into the pit, and

> locked and sealed it over him, so that he would deceive the nations no more, until the thousand years were ended. After that he must be let out for a little while.
>
> (Revelation 20.1–3)

This is exactly what happens when people repress evil, no matter how hard they try to contain it. Individual or group evil has to break out in the end. The devil is mighty hard to get rid of and pops up in the most unlikely places just when we thought we were finished with him! After *a little while* he joins his companions in the fiery lake, and we assume that is a fitting end to the deepest, darkest, unreformable evil.

Or is it? Most commentators assume that this lake is situated in some mythic underworld. But if this were so, it would leave some of creation unreconciled, and if God is to be 'all in all', and everything is to cohere in Christ, it would be contrary to the New Testament vision. In John's vision, there is a sea of glass, which represents the deep, incorporated into the worship and fabric of heaven. This feature had also been strangely represented on Sinai at the giving of the Ten Commandments, and in the inner courtyard of Solomon's temple (Exodus 24.10; 1 Kings 7.23–6). It reminded all who worshipped there of God's power over the *tehom* and could have added substance to the language of the psalms we have mentioned. In one passage of Revelation, this mysterious sea is mingled with fire, bubbling and spitting before the throne of God and those who have overcome the power of the devilish Domination System, in the heavenly counterpart of the temple:

> And I saw what appeared to be a sea of glass mingled with fire, and those who had conquered the beast and its image and the number of its name, standing beside the sea of glass with harps of God in their hands. And they sing . . .
>
> (Revelation 15.2–3)

Here is a vision of the deep mixed with a consuming fire which serves the purpose of God's holiness and justice. In the end God uses the powers which have brought evil to the world as the means by which they are destroyed. 'Satan sublimated, burning forever in the lake of fire, the crystal sea: transformation comes not through the denial and repression of our evil, but by naming it, owning it, and lifting it up to God.'[10] So what cannot be redeemed and brought within

God's loving purposes is brought before him to be burnt for ever. This raw, senseless and horrendous darkness is fired to blaze as an element of the eternal light – the best possible expression of the victory of God's unquenchable love over the deepest and blackest element of the deep.

Chapter 7

REDEEMING THE DEEP

Many waters cannot quench love, neither can floods drown it.

(Song of Songs 8.7)

In the story of the incarnation, crucifixion and resurrection of Jesus Christ, mythology and history come together to reveal God's plan to redeem the universe he created all along to be good. The whole beautiful cosmos is fallen, and has become a proud, oppressive self-confident system which imagines it can function independently of God's ways. We have described how this system manifests itself in systems of social, political, religious and economic power. We have seen how this system has a prince of its own, Satan as the devil, who has no more power than we give him by our complicity and collusion. All this marvellous design has been unravelled by sin and returns to *tohu wa-bohu*, unformed barren emptiness or chaos which must be redeemed.

Flesh

Our 'flesh' must be redeemed as well.[1] Flesh is the favourite word in the New Testament, especially in the Pauline letters, to describe human beings in their fallen state. Flesh has been taken captive by that very modern passion for personal satisfaction (Ephesians 2.3), and all other values which are not God's. The popular association of flesh with the the 'seven deadly sins' cripples us from having a proper New Testament understanding of the term.

Flesh includes every part of existence that humans have stamped their mark on. It includes the subtle 'power of the air' with its media overtones of Ephesians 2.2, which we take for granted because we grow up to assume its insidious validity without question. So it has community and environmental implications as well. The 'sins of the flesh' are not just private and personal, contrary to popular wisdom. They affect the way we think and work, the priorities we have, the advertisements we respond to, and the atmosphere we create and others create around us. Flesh includes fads of fashion, public opinion, peer pressure, ethnic and family loyalties, political propaganda and patriotic jingoism, media idols and hype, and 'assured proofs of science'. Everything in other words which determines our 'world view' unadjusted by the cosmic perspective of our Lord. This is 'the light' by which most people live, which paradoxically is the darkness that Jesus came to confront and overcome!

So what does redeemed 'flesh' look like? Because flesh is expressed in human bodily form, it cannot be redeemed without 'body'. Hence in Christian terms we look forward to the *redemption of our bodies* (Romans 8.23), not simply to a disembodied spiritual future as popularly supposed. And if, as some parts of the New Testament suggest, our immediate future beyond death is to experience some kind of disembodied intermediate state, this has to be suffered only until the end of this present age. Our destiny is to have a new spiritual body, and we show we believe it to be true by the way we treat our own bodies, and our relationships in community.

> What is sown is perishable, what is raised is imperishable. It is sown in dishonour, it is raised in glory. It is sown in weakness, it is raised in power. It is sown a physical body, it is raised a spiritual body. If there is a physical body, there is also a spiritual body.
>
> (1 Corinthians 15.42–4)

Time

Time has fallen too, so that it becomes an oppressive enemy as well. We cannot 'afford' the time to do what we ought to, because time costs money. We speak of time 'catching up with us', as though another escape strategy has failed. We spend a fortune on the latest time-saving gadgets. We educate our children into this sense of bondage, which they are not born with (watch young children playing, oblivious of time!). Parents bully them with 'It's time to . . .' many times a day. And how they hate 'It's time for bed!' By contrast, we can appear to have too much time. We are tempted to waste time and 'kill' it. Boredom is a modern disease of a society obsessed with the need to pack as much into every minute as possible. Then, the battle of ageing is fought with fanatical energy by a civilization that pretends technology can produce immortality. Hundreds of millions of pounds are spent on cosmetic products designed to disguise the passing of time. Time is about decay, and death is its greatest victory.

Little wonder then that Jesus describes this present 'age' as marked by the cares and desires which choke the message that could bring liberation (Mark 4.19). We forget that time, represented by the 'days' of creation, was originally good. Time has fallen to become another of the most fiercely oppressive of powers like the rest of the cosmos. If we have tasted the powers of the age to come, we are called to co-operate with this redemptive process – *redeeming the time* (Ephesians 4.16 AV).

God's plan of redemption

In his life, death and rising, Jesus Christ conquers the principalities and powers which hold the universe in its grip. He becomes 'flesh', the symbol of our human existence, and becomes subject to time, so that he can redeem it. In short, God in Christ redeems the universe *from within*. The symbolism of the deep underlies the story of the cross, just as it does the creation, the fall, the flood, and the history of the nation of Israel.

Tom Wright, interpreting Jesus' true vocation, has written of the events of the cross, 'Jesus reconstrued the battle which had to be fought as the battle against the real enemy, the accuser, the Satan. He renounced the battle that his contemporaries expected a Messiah to fight, and that several would-be Messiahs in that century were only too eager to fight. He faced, instead, what he seems to have conceived as the battle against the forces of darkness, standing behind the visible forces (both Roman and Jewish) ranged against him.'[2] The cross would be the means of the victory of God. Paul works out the consequences of this conquest in his letters. In Colossians 1 and 2, Christ is described as *head of all rule* (i.e. rules, rituals and belief systems) *and authority* – the spiritual power that gives them the ability to impose themselves on peoples' lives (Colossians 2.10). All these 'rulers and authorities', systems, the fallen pattern of human societies, and time itself, have been disarmed of their power by the victory of Christ on the cross:

> God made you alive together with him, when he forgave us all our trespasses, erasing the record that stood against us with its legal demands. He set this aside, nailing it to the cross. He disarmed the

rulers and authorities and made a public example of them, triumphing over them in it.

(Colossians 2.13b–15)

When we come to feel the truth of Paul's marvellous vision in our bones, and not just in our heads, there is an immense experience of physical and psychological health and liberation. The victory of Christ can set us free from the power of these insistently godlike norms, demands and institutions like nothing else. We can stop living an inauthentic 'dominated' existence where our whole identity depends on satisfying other peoples' expectations, and start to discover who we really are. Of course, Satan and his minions are still all around us, full of fight. They wait to be completely redeemed, or, if they are unredeemable, to be subsumed into the purposes of God (1 Corinthians 15.24–8). But the decisive battle with these powers of the deep has been won, and it is this victory which makes possible the reconciliation of human beings and the whole cosmos to God and his purposes. So Paul declares in his great hymn

. . . at the name of Jesus every knee should bend,
in heaven and on earth and under the earth,
and every tongue should confess that Jesus Christ is Lord,
to the glory of God the Father.

(Philippians 2.10–11)

No one theory in itself is adequate to describe what God has done for us in Jesus Christ. Theories are about explaining facts. The cross of Christ is history but it is more than a historical fact. Like the creation and the fall, it is a theological revelation in vivid pictures, a parable in images which will never go out of date and whose meaning cannot be conveyed by facts alone. It is beyond the aims of this book to explore the wealth of metaphors expressing the meaning of the cross in the New Testament. But there are three other ideas which specially relate the theology of the deep to the life, death and rising of Jesus Christ.

1 The deep in Jesus' baptism

Just as he was coming up out of the water, he saw the heavens torn apart and the Spirit descending like a dove on him. And a voice came from heaven, 'You are my Son, the Beloved; with you I am well pleased.' And the Spirit immediately drove him out into the wilderness.

(Mark 1.10–12; and see parallels)

We have here an amazing concentration of Old Testament images. First, *the creation story* with the *tehom* represented by the river Jordan, and the brooding Spirit of God with the creative word interacting with the receptive heart of Jesus to begin a new creation. Jesus is to be the first-born representative of all the many who through the action of water and Spirit will be made part of this new world that God is fashioning out of the failures and disasters of the old.

The story of the Flood is echoed at the Baptism. Here Jesus is representative of humankind. He is pictured as going down into the deep which now is a symbol of judgement. As at the Flood in Genesis 8, the dove heralds the dawn of new beginnings for humanity and the wider cosmos, as Jesus comes up out of the water. The dove is also a reminder of *the story of Jonah*. Jesus is commissioned for his missionary ministry by the action of a *yonah* (dove). He is to be a 'dove-person'. In other words his calling is to announce God's mercy to the gentiles as well as the Jews, something the original Jonah, representing Old Testament Judaism, lamentably failed to do.[3]

What of the association of the words spoken to Jesus? 'You are my Son, the Beloved' echoes Psalm 2, with all its overtones of the victory of a king of David's line over his enemies. 'With you I am well pleased' comes from Isaiah 42. God's missionary is to be his gentle, humble, suffering servant. He will not bruise or beat the reluctant into submission like many evangelists down the centuries!

Finally *the Exodus story* is clearly represented at the Baptism. The Exodus marks the birth of the nation from slavery. Jesus, the faithful representative Israelite, makes the journey through the waters to the new promised land, led by the Spirit of God through the wilderness. Later on, Luke records Jesus looking forward to the events in Jerusalem as another mighty *exodos* (Luke 9.31, Greek), where the battle he will wage with the religious and civil authorities will be like a contest with a latter-day Pharaoh. His baptism at the Jordan river is then an acted parable in the true tradition of the Old Testament prophets – nothing less than prophetic anticipation of his death in Jerusalem at the climax of his ministry. The baptism of the Holy Spirit is also then a baptism of suffering. All three Synoptic Gospels go on to report Jesus' words linking baptism with his death, a work which must be shared with his disciples

> I have a baptism with which to be baptized, and what stress I am under until it is completed!
>
> (Luke 12.50)

> Jesus said to them, 'The cup that I drink you will drink, and with the baptism with which I am baptized, you will be baptized.
>
> (Mark 10.39)

In Jesus' baptism then, all the three elements of the deep we have identified are present, the water, the desert, and the darkness of death. His baptism-in-death will be like the victory over the mighty *tehom* at the Red Sea, when those enslaved to the oppressive, life-denying powers of the present age, who come with him will be set free. An Easter hymn expresses the symbolism:

> Come ye faithful, raise the strain
> of triumphant gladness;
> God hath brought his Israel
> into joy from sadness;
> Loosed from Pharaoh's bitter yoke
> Jacob's sons and daughters;
> Led them with unmoistened foot
> Through the Red Sea waters.[4]

2 The deep in the darkness at the crucifixion

Jesus of Nazareth died at Passover time outside the city wall in Jerusalem around 30 CE. The crucifixion account is divided by the sentence

> When it was noon, darkness came over the whole land until three in the afternoon.
>
> (Mark 15.33)

Between the third and the sixth hour, there is a great deal of movement, violent reaction and mockery when Jesus utters no word at all. After the period of darkness at the ninth hour, there is the appalling shout, 'My God, my God why have you forsaken me?' A great cry of abandonment bursts from Jesus before he dies, while bystanders scurry around in a futile way like headless chickens. Those three hours of darkness in the middle of the day are unprecedented. The 'deep-as-darkness' would appear to have won the battle as the beauty and power of God in Jesus is crushed by the religious and civil authorities. Or, to put it in St John's language, the light of the world is extinguished by the uncomprehending darkness.

At the very beginning of the cosmos, light followed the darkness. As the drama of the cross is played out, it is as though the creation story is being rewound again to the beginning, and everything returned to its primal state. At the ninth hour, when the light appears, God is saying again, 'Let there be light!' (Genesis 1.3), and a new ordering of creation begins. The Son of Man thus endures the darkness of the *tehom* to bring a new beginning for us, and for the whole universe. 'Here is the God who controls the waters and the power of darkness – the creator who is at the same time the redeemer. Myth and historical event are here used together, so that the event and its meaning are one.'[5]

3 Jesus' descent into hell

It is easy to skip over the familiar words 'He descended into hell' in the creeds, without thinking. In this phrase is a wonderful mystery illustrating another facet of the cross of Christ. The parable of Jesus' 'descent' into hell is the logical consequence of his incarnation, but it did not just occur in the time frame between his death and resurrection that first Easter morning. It began when he became a human being. When he 'pitched his tent' (John 1.14) amidst a fallen world, so that the evangelists could testify that they had seen nothing less than the glory of God in him.

Jesus went to hellish places

His life on earth began in a cold draughty insanitary rock cave. He travelled with his parents as a refugee child to Egypt and back to flee from the jealous rage of Herod. Before he began his public ministry, he spent forty days without food in the awful semi-desert of Judaea, overlooking the Dead Sea, where it was baking hot by day and near-freezing by night. During the course of his three-year ministry he lived on the streets and in the open air with his disciples. He entered infectious leper colonies, endured life-threatening boat journeys by night on the Sea of Galilee, visited tombs like those of the demonized man and of Lazarus. He endured the desolation of Gethsemane, the hostile atmosphere of the Sanhedrin, the scourging and agony of the Via Dolorosa, and the ghastly painful isolation and degradation of Golgotha, where he was crucified. In that short three-year ministry, Jesus endured hellish places; lonely, cold, hostile places of death.

Jesus ministered to people in a hell of their own

The demonized looked to him for release from their prison. The chronically sick sought him out endlessly for healing from their never-ending weakness. Diseased lepers and the prostitutes, despised and ostracized, looked to him for a touch to bring humanity, relationship, forgiveness and hope. The blind looked to him to restore their eyes in their darkness. The socially excluded – women, children, Samaritans and gentiles – looked to him for friendship and human dignity. John the Baptist looked to him for reassurance in prison for being obedient to God's will. The dying thief on the cross looked to him for a future. All these suffered their own brand of hell. Jesus embodied what he preached. He forsook the splendour of the highest heaven by being born a true humble human being, taking the form of Isaiah's suffering servant. He gave his life to the world in sacrifice by going into hell with humanity.

Jesus truly died and was buried

Death, disintegration, utter lifelessness is part of our understanding of the *tehom*. Jesus died after about six hours on the cross, earlier than the authorities expected, but hardly surprising in view of the circumstances of his trial and scourging. This made it unnecessary for the soldiers to hasten his end by breaking his legs. Crucifixion was commonplace, and Roman soldiers were expert executioners. The flow of blood and water showed they knew which part of the body to pierce with the spear, either to extinguish all remaining life, or to ensure their victim was dead. He was then buried in a rock tomb, and his body bound with strips of cloth heavy with spices.

O Death, Death, He is come.
O grounds of Hell make room.

Who came from further than the stars
Now comes as low beneath.
Thy ribbed ports, O Death
Make wide; and Thou, O Lord of Sin,
Lay open thine estates.
Lift up your heads, O Gates;
Be ye lift up, ye everlasting doors
The King of Glory will come in.[6]

Hell

Gerard Manley Hopkins shows us graphically how poetry can be the link between physical events and experience and the metaphysical or spiritual state of a concept like hell or Sheol. The Bible uses its own poetry to make the same kind of links all the time. When Jesus died the belief is he entered Sheol. Sheol for the Jews, known as Hades to the Greeks, was never a place of total extinction. It was, as we saw in the Psalms, a place of non-being, an underworld of shadows, misery and futility – a land of silence and forgottenness, which could be anticipated through experience and circumstances in life. It does not carry the 'hell-fire' overtones of final punishment of the wicked in mythic fiery Gehenna, which developed among the Pharisees in the last centuries before Christ along with ideas of bodily resurrection. When the creeds refer to the descent into hell, it is Sheol or Hades which is referred to, more specifically, *place of departed spirits*. A profound and imaginative treatment of the idea of Sheol is given in C. S. Lewis's *The Great Divorce*.[7]

In Peter's first sermon on the day of Pentecost, he draws on Psalm 16 as an assurance that God did not abandon Jesus' soul in Hades (Acts 2.27). He elaborates this thought in the course of his first letter:

> He was put to death in the flesh, but made alive in the spirit, in which also he went and made a proclamation to the spirits in prison, who in former times did not obey, when God waited patiently in the days of Noah, during the building of the ark ... this is the reason the gospel was proclaimed even to the dead, so that, though they had been judged in the flesh as everyone is judged, they might live in the spirit as God does.
>
> (1 Peter 3.18–20; 4.6)

Commentators down the centuries have struggled with the identity of the 'spirits in prison'.[8] Were they just the band of fallen angels, Titans, half-gods, half-men referred to before the Flood in Genesis 6? If so, what was Jesus proclaiming to them? Two different Greek words translate 'proclaim' in our Bibles, of which only the second means 'declare the good news'? So some believe the 'spirits in prison' are these wicked angels who hear the bad news of their final doom. This is a perfectly reasonable interpretation of the passage if it is assumed that Genesis 6.1–4 refers to actual antediluvian history.

But suppose that these ideas are couched in the language of parable and theology as most believe. Then we have in Genesis 6.1–4 another version of the Fall and its consequences. Now the Fall is not confined to the 'earth' of Adam and Eve and their successors, but includes the 'heaven' of the angels. The union of heaven and earth described there produces a mighty all-conquering insolent race of godlike people. This is not just about ancient civilizations. It is about the history of the human race. Genesis 6 has equally uncomfortable modern overtones in Fascist philosophies like Nazism, or the current disturbing prospect of widespread genetic mutation. Or it can be represented by today's modern political and economic titans, where sexual prowess is clearly allied to the lust for power and domination; or by any generation, in fact, self-consciously and arrogantly 'come of age' which thinks it can live life without reference to God. Only God's power can release these people from their prisons!

So it is reasonable to link these verses together, and take Jesus Christ's preaching to the dead to heart. Peter's 'spirits in prison' are not just fallen angels getting their just deserts in mythic dungeons, but anyone and everyone imprisoned for whatever reason by hostile life-denying forces within or outside themselves in this life, as well as beyond death. We have outlined the way Jesus preached the good news to many 'spirits in prison' during the course of his earthly ministry. Peter reminds us in his letter that Jesus continued this liberating ministry in Hades. And Ephesians 4.8 implies that Jesus left nothing in the cosmos unvisited from heights to depths, *making captivity captive* as he 'ascends' to take his place above the heavens 'at God's right hand'!

At the end of Chapter 4, we explored the way God could be present in our experience of deep depression through the prayers of the Psalmist. In this remarkable picture of Christ's descent into hell, our Lord actually comes and announces that we can be redeemed and rescued in the prisons we have made for ourselves, or others have put us in. As someone who has been prone to bouts of depression throughout my adult life, I can identify with those words. Feelings of sad, agitated exhaustion, coupled with intense waves of badness that seem to pour over my innermost soul in floods, plunging me downwards into a spiral of blackness.

This periodic and overwhelming feeling of worthlessness has not been helped by the understanding of the cross I embraced as a young man, because it was the approved way in to Christian faith and the fellowship of the Church then. I have always loved singing hymns, and as a parish priest I try to work with all sorts, ancient and modern, creatively in worship. Yet I came to the point of wanting to make a violent and angry protest at Victorian hymns and many modern songs which concentrate on ecstatically praising Jesus for his marvellous sinlessness, at the same time morbidly meditating on how terribly sinful and wicked *we* are. Christ was everything and I was nothing, and this was supposed to be good! Such expressions of piety are written from the highest motives, and are true to the faith in one way. But they just serve to drive the knife in if we are tempted from time to time to accept the blame for the ills of the whole world!

I remember asking for hands to be laid on me during prayer at a time of worship at a conference I had organized. I admitted to God in the silence that I was utterly exhausted trying to make myself valuable to other people. Everyone was singing at length about Christ and the benefits of his crucifixion all around me, but I was the one who was being crucified! I felt intensely angry because the faith that I was called to commend was being experienced as life-denying rather than life-affirming. My anger just intensified the sense of guilt. I felt suffocated and found it physically very difficult to breathe. I then had a mental picture of myself as I was then sitting, with my head bowed in prayer. This picture gradually became smaller and smaller, and as it did so, I became foetus-like, and gradually disappeared to become a tiny dot. I was nothing. It was an extraordinary regression into the womb. At this point I 'heard' an inner voice saying quite distinctly, 'I have been crucified with you.'

In life, no house, no home
my Lord on earth might have.
In death, no friendly tomb

but what a stranger gave.
What may I say?
Heaven was his home;
but mine the tomb
wherein he lay.[9]

After the prayers ended, I thanked my colleagues, and went straight off to bed. I became very calm and immediately went into a deep sleep. Next morning, while half-awake, I had another mental picture. I was walking alone in a warm featureless desert-like but not unpleasant place where the sand-dunes stretched for miles in all directions. Then I remember wondering which way to explore. It did not matter which way I went. I was free to go whichever way I liked, and when I had time to recover from the physical and mental exhaustion I felt incredibly liberated by the experience. I read Psalm 116

For you have delivered my soul from death,
my eyes from tears, my feet from stumbling.
I walk before the Lord in the land of the living

(Psalm 116.8–9)

An empathic understanding of the cross

I shall explore the meaning of this experience a little more in the following chapter. For now, let us try to understand Christ's cross as expressed by the words 'I have been crucified with you.' I was surprised at the time, because I had always been brought up to believe and sing hymns about Christ dying *instead of* me.

This insight into the meaning of the cross has strong echoes of Jürgen Moltmann's great book *The Crucified God* (SCM, 1974). Moltmann contrasts the God of the Bible, capable of suffering because he is capable of life, with the Greek gods, which were incapable of feeling anything.

We have already noted the conflict in the heart of God before he commanded the *tehom* to return in the judgement of the flood. In Hosea 11, there is another expression of the agony in God's heart over the apostasy of the Northern Kingdom of Israel

How can I give you up, Ephraim? How can I hand you over, O Israel?

> ...
> My heart recoils within me; my compassion grows warm
> and tender.
> I will not execute my fierce anger; I will not again
> destroy Ephraim;
> for I am God and no mortal, the Holy One in your midst,
> and I will not come in wrath.
>
> (Hosea 11.8–9)

Any loving parent will be able to identify with these feelings over the actions of a wayward offspring. 'At the centre of the Christian faith is a history: the history of the passion,'[10] both passionate love and anguish. Jesus, he says, was no dumb sheep submitting to a distressing fate, but a human being who suffered the full pains of an agonizing rejection and death. Jesus went against the modern trend of anaesthetizing pain. He felt the full force of the crown of thorns and the nails. Moltmann illustrates this first with the story of *Gethsemane*. Jesus' passion to do his Father's will, and to further the Kingdom agenda of liberating the captives, healing the sick, embracing the outcasts, and forgiving the guilty, brought him up against the full force of the opposition. Before the military arrive in the garden, as Jesus comes face to face with his impending fate, he asks for the cup of suffering to be taken from him (Mark 14.36). God for the first time we know is silent, and it is here that Jesus' passion really begins. This is the first time his fellowship with his heavenly Father is broken and his oneness with the Father is shattered. This is the real reason for those huge tear drops. Jesus is confronting the deep – something the great Christian saints like St John of the Cross have experienced similarly, in the 'dark night of the soul'. Others of us have felt it as unanswered prayer. Here, Jesus is not just struggling with himself. He is struggling with an unaccustomed experience of God as deaf, or apparently absent.

In the experience of *Golgotha*, before Jesus dies, his last words to the God he has been so intimate with are 'My God, my God, why have you forsaken me?' (Mark 15.34). At the centre of our faith is a God-forsaken cry. The cry of the tortured, the disillusioned, the faithless in the light of appalling suffering. This is no prayer of trust to *Abba* of the Lord's Prayer, but an agonized shout of betrayal to a deity who had let him down in his hour of need. Jesus himself had his doubts, big ones, as he hung on that cruel cross. 'Is this the end of every human faith in God, or is it the beginning of that reborn faith which can no longer be shaken by anything at all? The passionately loving Christ, the persecuted Christ, the lonely Christ, the tortured Christ, the Christ who suffers under God's silence – this is our brother. But where is God? Apparently nowhere!'[11]

So why did God abandon Jesus on the cross?

It was out of passionate love for us. Moltmann goes on to point out that when Christ, God's Son, suffers death, the Father of Jesus Christ suffers his forsakenness by the Son. Both suffer, in different ways. Christ's passion becomes God's passion. 'God was in Christ' (2 Corinthians 5.19), so God too experiences death on the cross. God goes with us. Where Christ, God's Son, goes, he reminds us, God the Father goes too. Where then is God, in the silence of the cross? Amazingly, and mysteriously in the dying Christ. Because Christ is truly human with us. He is our brother among brothers and sisters. God empties himself too in this movement towards us, in the way the passion story develops. With each indignity during the arrest, trial, walk to the place of execution, and crucifixion, Christ goes 'lower and lower' and God is there with him, in the depths.

Jürgen Moltmann's interpretation of the cross is so fresh, and speaks to where many people are today. Christ's cross stands with the countless other crosses inflicted down the centuries on the victims of the oppressive powers of religion, politics, race, culture, family, sexual prejudice and the like. God in Jesus Christ became humiliated and forsaken because the cosmic powers wanted to be rid of him. So now he can be a brother to the humiliated and forsaken as well. He will not miraculously deliver Jesus from the pains of the cross as the crowds taunted him on that dreadful day. He delivers through his wounds. God is on the side of the victims.

The groaning of creation,
wrung out by pain and care,
the anguish of a million hearts
that break in dumb despair;
O crucified redeemer,
these are thy cries of pain;
O may they break our selfish hearts,
and love come in to reign.[12]

Christ is our redeemer too. There is no forgiveness of guilt without some kind of atonement. It cost Jesus Christ to release us. In Isaiah 53.4 we read, 'Surely he has borne our infirmities, and carried our diseases'. In the experience of the cross, God carries the sins of the people, and so transforms our suffering into his own. 'In Christ, God did not die for individual sins, but by bearing and enduring US! He died not so much for our individual sins, but for us sinners! By being for us, Christ makes it plain that God is for us too.'[13]

None of us can grasp the immense mystery and wonder of the cross of Christ. After all the cross is for the world, and not just for one person. Each one of us needs a way to see in the darkness, and to understand how God in Christ has redeemed the deep *from within.* I find these insights into the great parable of the cross health-giving and liberating. Christ has won the victory over the powerful forces and powerful people that oppress. To achieve this he goes down to the depths to release the spirits who have been put in prison by them or the spirits who are there because of their own stubbornness and disobedience. He suffers and dies with us, so that from this encounter with the deep, new life, new hope, and indeed a new world, may be born.

Chapter 8

THE TOMB AND THE WOMB OF THE DEEP

Long my imprisoned spirit lay
Fast bound in sin and nature's night;
Thine eye diffused a quickening ray,
I woke, the dungeon flamed with light;
My chains fell off; my heart was free;
I rose, went forth, and followed thee.[1]

In his imaginative book *Four Gospels, One Jesus?*, Richard Burridge writes of John's Gospel, 'It is not enough to explain Jesus in human origins of time or place or ancestry, since he exists from before all time. In the beginning he was with God, and he is God . . . John's story of Jesus is nothing less than a life of the cosmos.'[2] John begins his Gospel as a deliberate parallel to the creation story of Genesis 1. The coming of Jesus the incarnate Word of God means nothing less than a new creation for the flawed and stained universe. This creation emphasis extends through the Gospel. It is there at the beginning of chapter 3, where Jesus puzzles Nicodemus, a considerable intellect in his own right, as he describes the way to enter into the kingdom of God.

> [Nicodemus] came to Jesus by night and said to him, 'Rabbi, we know that you are a teacher who has come from God; for no one can do these signs that you do apart from the presence of God.' Jesus answered him, 'Very truly, I tell you, no one can see the kingdom of God without being born from above.' Nicodemus said to him, 'How can anyone be born after having grown old? Can one enter a second time into the mother's womb and be born?' Jesus answered, 'Very truly, I tell you, no one can enter the kingdom of God without being born of water and Spirit.'
>
> (John 3.2–5)

Exploring Nicodemus' question

Preachers often make the point that Nicodemus came by night because he was afraid of what his colleagues might say if they knew he had been meeting Jesus. That may well be, but for John, the faith of Pharisees, though light to them, was in fact darkness compared with the light now shining in Jesus. So we have here another creation scene, with the darkness, the wind of the Spirit, which blows where it chooses, and the symbolic water. The creative intent of God is implied in the birthing process, and that lovely ambiguous Greek word *anothen* ('from above', or 'again') tells us where the initiative is coming from. How else can Nicodemus be part of God's 'system', his kingdom, unless he is transformed in his whole personality through a movement of the Holy Spirit over his own dark cosmos?

The Bible is full of references to the endlessly creative and re-creative power of God. Sometimes it is difficult to distinguish between what 'the above' is creating, fresh, newly-minted and original as though it had never appeared before, and what God is re-making 'again' after the original has been spoiled. Redemption is another word for re-creation. We *experience* the difference in that 'before and after' awareness of the touch of God's Spirit, but from God's point of view this process is part of the growing pains as he fashions his creation towards its appointed goal.

> We know that the whole creation has been groaning in labour pains until now; and not only the creation, but we ourselves, who have the first fruits of the Spirit, groan inwardly while we wait for adoption, the redemption of our bodies.
>
> (Romans 8.22–3)

We have already noted how God renewed creation after the parable of the Flood, and in the story of the crucifixion. And how he recreated the nation he had lovingly birthed in the Exodus story, after the exile. In the encounter with Nicodemus, Jesus is speaking of what he can do for individuals, using the same creation symbolism. The unformed cosmos at the beginning is pictured like an immense dark, watery womb waiting to give birth to light and myriad forms of life through the brooding gale of the Spirit. In the same way, the human female womb is a kind of cosmos, bringing new life to birth through water and the Spirit. The parallel is not so far-fetched. When Job rues the day he was born, he describes his own birth in precisely the same terms, and wishes that the creation process had been reversed, in dark poetry!

> Let the day perish in which I was born . . . Let that day be darkness!
> May God above not seek it . . . Let gloom and deep darkness claim it.
> Let clouds settle upon it . . . Yes, let that night be barren;
> . . .
> Let those curse it who curse the Sea,
> those who are skilled to rouse up Leviathan.
> . . .
> because it did not shut the doors of my mother's womb,
> and hide trouble from my eyes.
>
> (Job 3.3–10)

Womb and tomb

Those passages which speak of Jeremiah being known by God before he formed him in the womb (Jeremiah 1 .5), and the suffering servant who is to be a *light to the nations* being called and named in his mother's womb (Isaiah 49.1–6) come from a similar source. So does Luke's account of the Spirit overshadowing Mary before the birth of Jesus. What God is forming secretly in the dark he will bring forth for all to see. Jesus' encounter with Nicodemus taps a rich vein of images of creation and the deep. At the end of John's Gospel, in a wonderful piece of symbolism, Jesus' body is buried in Nicodemus' tomb. So in the sequence incarnation–crucifixion–resurrection, the womb and the tomb, both enclosing the uncreated deep 'non-being' of the *tehom*, become the place of new creation, or 'being' through the power of the Spirit of God.

Born again?

At the end of the last chapter I recounted a little of my own spiritual and psychological experience of the 'tomb', which also turned out to be a profound regression to the womb. I want to give an explanation of my own experience described there. I shall show how it links up with the thinking outlined above in John 3, particularly the meaning of the phrase to be *born from above*, or 'born again'. This phrase has been hijacked and devalued by thoughtless and superficial use in evangelistic jargon. It is also used to validate Christian credentials in transatlantic political soundbites. The result has been that countless good Christians protest that they don't believe in 'born-again Christianity', which is a pity when really they are complaining about the way this phrase about being-in-Christ is casually thrown around. And the baggage which is usually implied with it, which includes demands for evidence of instant and dramatic conversion experiences! To be 'born again' or *born from above* is a special Johannine insight into the process of embracing the life and the values of Christ and his kingdom. It must be redeemed as a valid and healthy theological way of expressing Christian experience.

Regeneration and conversion

John 3 is not an isolated account of the difference the Holy Spirit will make to the followers of Jesus. At the first Pentecost, the rushing mighty creative wind of the Holy Spirit made new people of the first apostles and their friends. Although the exact word *palingenesia* ('Genesis all over again') occurs only twice,[3] Paul, Peter and James in their letters speak in different ways of being a new creation in Jesus Christ, so that the original image of the Creator is being restored in us (Colossians 3.10). Christian people are the first-fruits of the new age which has broken into the existing order through Jesus and the Spirit. Regeneration, or 'born again-ness' is something that only God can do. Our response, what we do, must be to turn (i.e. to convert or repent) and 'become like little children' (Matthew 18.3; Mark 10.15) or 'babes in arms' (Luke 18.15–16) – the Synoptic equivalent of John's new-birth imagery. Becoming and being a Christian, then, is not first of all about morality, contrary to popular perception. It is our response to God's cosmic regeneration, accomplished through Jesus Christ's coming.

Jesus our model for humanity

The title Son of Man is used of Jesus Christ 82 times in the New Testament, all but one in the Gospels. It is by a long way his preferred title when he refers to himself. In the book of Daniel chapter 7 and a few places in the Gospels it is a glorious Messianic title. But the Hebrew phrase corresponding to Son of Man is *bar adam*, which just means 'human being'. Jesus is the true *Adam* understood now not just in parable but in flesh and blood, visible for all to see. God begins the process of cosmic regeneration in the Gospel story by showing us his glory in humanity through the Incarnation. Jesus is *the* human being as God has designed us to be. He is our model for human life and human relationships. One of Frank Lake's special legacies to our understanding of human personality is the Dynamic Cycle of interpersonal relationships that he developed in discussion with the Swiss theologian Emil Brunner.[4]

From a study of John's Gospel, Lake shows how there are four distinct phases in the dynamic cycle of relationships that Jesus enjoyed. First, his essential Being, the knowledge of who he is, derives from an intimate relationship he has with his Father, whose love is constantly mediated to him by the Holy Spirit. Through this intimacy, to which he has instant access through prayer, Jesus finds *Acceptance*.

Acceptance produces a sense of identity and well-being, as Jesus is united with his Father from day to day in prayer and worship. This gives him *Sustenance*, and brings out of him an overflow of love and joy, grace and truth. From this well-being flows a sense of *Status* which gives him confidence to do his Father's will throughout his ministry. He loves people as he himself has been loved. Finally his ministry gives him a sense of *Achievement*, as he does only what his Father wants, in being the light of the world, fulfilling his destiny as God's Son in redemption and sacrifice. The cycle is repeated again and again, as during the stresses and human demands of his ministry he returns to his Father to pour his heart out, and to find renewed Acceptance and strength for his task.

We can represent Frank Lake's dynamic cycle of relationships very simply:

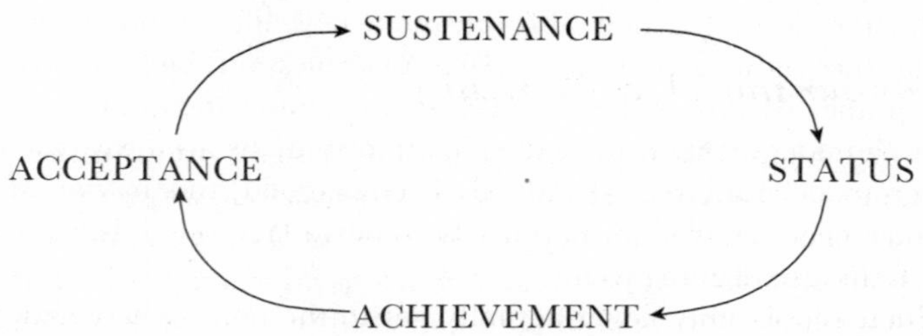

Jesus' life gives us a splendid integrated picture of what human beings are designed to be in their essential personality. He shows us too such openness in his prayer life with *Abba*, his Father, and in his daily relationships with his disciples and all who meet him. Every child needs to be engaged in a similar dynamic relational cycle from the beginning, to grow up healthy and well-adjusted:

- *Acceptance* – experiencing parental delight as a gift, expressed in a sense of happiness, relaxed freedom, safety, and non-judgemental care.
- *Sustenance* – particularly feeding, and the way food is given, putting the person in the centre, and attending to their wider needs with quality and reliability.
- *Status* follows naturally from this experience, building up a sense of 'all-rightness' and positive identity, knowing who they are and what their role is in life. Finally,
- *Achievement* springs from a sense of good status. The young person can begin to explore their own abilities and the world around with confidence. There needs of course to be an awareness of boundaries, because no one can be omnipotent, but boundaries can be relaxed as self-control develops. Such experience leads to trust with healthy reactions when things go wrong. That takes the cycle back to forgiveness and new beginnings again, but with all the wealth of experience and sense of worth obtained in the earlier journey.[5]

This ideal pattern inevitably does not work as smoothly in a fallen world, even with the best possible start. There are an endless number of variables playing on parents and children at each stage of the nurturing and growing process. If for whatever reason it is not possible or easy for parents to accept the new life they have in their arms, things go wrong from the start. An unwanted or resented child, for example, inevitably means a new life cannot begin the cycle the right way round. Any awareness of lack of love or acceptance by any of the key players in a child's life at any stage in growth may quickly lead to the idea that humans need to achieve in order to be noticed and valued. Feeling good and having status among peers as well as parents becomes a perilous business even when things are going well.

Such people may never actually get to the point where they can accept themselves and be free, relaxed, and content at all. So the dynamic cycle is reversed, to become:

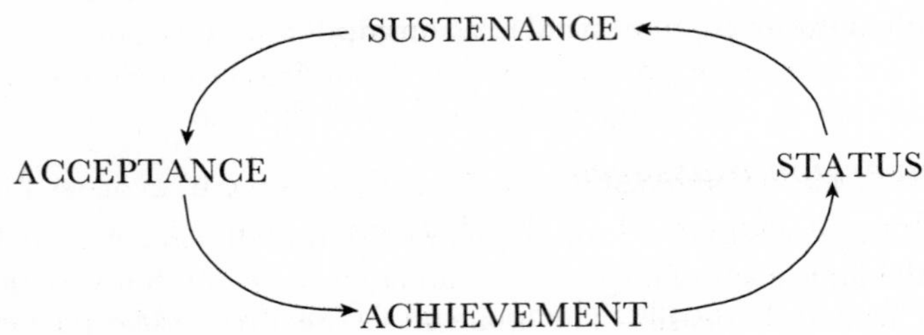

Modern Western thinking tends to undervalue parenthood, to farm children out at the earliest possible opportunity, and to promote an overdeveloped work ethic. The importance of play is underappreciated. Toys have to be consciously 'educational' to be thought worthwhile buying from the age of three. Even playtime at school gets cut out so that academic performance fits the Ofsted inspectors' criteria and those of discerning parents, comparing schools in the local education 'market'. Even sport is a 'business' and has ceased to be fun any more, because everyone loves a winner. Winners get star treatment by the media. Success is celebrated in banner headlines. Competition is intense – even on TV game shows! And failures are sidelined and rejected.

Even when children are born into families where they are warmly accepted and nurtured, the pervasive influence of the visual images on television acts as an all-powerful surrogate parent. Many children enjoy more hours of cradling and nurture in the violent hero-takes-all philosophy of television cartoons than they enjoy in their own parents' company. They are reminded from a very early age that 'good' people have to achieve things, pass exams, be a winner and be successful, and even on occasions be violent, in order to have 'street cred' with their peers. We are what we earn and what we buy! Only if we do will we have status. Only when we have status will we be able to accept ourselves for what we are. How many achieve *that*? It is easy to see we are in the world of the Domination System described in Chapter 5, and here are some of its insidious personal origins. Parents, children and teachers and television producers breathe its poisonous oppressive atmosphere every day and accept it as the natural way of the world. They unwittingly perpetuate these attitudes across the generations, even though they might privately protest and wonder where it is all leading. No one grows up unscathed. Most end up casualties of the 'System', damaged in health and scarred in personal relationships.

Conversion massaged

Jesus' answer is that we must turn around, literally, and start to live the dynamic cycle of life the truly human way he did. But we cannot turn around that easily. The oppressive system tries to keep beating us into its dehumanizing mould. So 'turning to Christ' can be made to appear like turning to a religious paddle when the demands of the System are getting too close for comfort. We may turn, yes, but we do not change our basic direction in life. That remains devoted to status, sustenance of our image, and acceptance as the great reward for all our efforts! The temptation is to take faith on board and simply make it part of the success story which will improve our overall image. And so media hype comes to church – where conversions are dramatic, healings are spectacular, and people making something of life are flocking to churches which preach what they want to hear. Nothing succeeds like success in Christian circles. Unfortunately there is no room for casualties in this religious version of the Domination System. After all, it crucified our Lord!

Worse still, if we understand that acceptance is a reward for achieving whatever society decides is 'good', acceptance by God becomes conditional, not absolute. We forget God loves all that he has made, without 'ifs' and 'buts'. We are ashamed of the bad side of ourselves, with its sin, weaknesses and failures. Naturally we prefer to own our 'successes' in a success-dominated society. So we are tempted to adopt well-worn strategems to clean up our image before God as well as before others. We can deny our 'badness' if it is only something we are privately aware of, splitting it off from other more presentable parts of our life, and burying it deep in our unconscious, on the 'out of sight out of mind' principle. Where our sins and failures are public knowledge, we can project the blame – or the sin itself – onto other people. If we come really unstuck, then we can blame the devil! That works particularly well in some Christian circles where the devil has a high profile in their spiritual thinking. Everyone colludes with the idea, because they're all doing the same thing! As well as blaming the devil they may themselves be projecting the blame for their own failures onto us, and if we have no clear idea what is going on and how to resist it, we can end up bearing a whole load of false guilt as well.

This process of splitting, evasion and projection expends an enormous amount of spiritual and mental energy, most of which we are not aware of because it becomes second nature until we suffer nervous exhaustion. At best, our innermost selves are impoverished and divided deep within so that we cease to speak, think and act with integrity. At worst, we can become anxious, insecure and severely depressed. We do not feel accepted by God or anyone else, even though we make strenuous efforts to achieve the good required by what we judge to be their fierce expectations. We cannot accept ourselves either, because the lawless elements of lust, anger and greed within the split-off areas of our consciousness continue to rage deep within us. Hell and the tomb are not far away. Paul knew all about this when he wrote

> So I find it to be a law that when I want to do what is good, evil lies close at hand. For I delight in the law of God in my inmost self, but I see in my members another law at war with the law of my mind, making me captive to the law of sin that dwells in my members. Wretched man that I am! Who will rescue me from this body of death?
>
> (Romans 7.21–4)

True conversion

All the time, our Lord is inviting us to something as radical as life and death, because *this body of death* has to die. It is anxious, divided, exhausted, defeated and terrified, all at once. From being a tiny baby, having a profound integrity at birth, we have become part of the chaos of the *tehom* again, tossed around by its waves.[6] And the wonder is that our Lord has been there in the chaos before us through the experience of his cross. He has been down to the darkest, deepest hell, and is able to share our hellish experiences too.

The New Testament makes it clear there is no eternal future in believing that God's acceptance can only come through work and achievement, although millions pursue it like eager lemmings. To quote Paul again, we need to 'be renewed in the spirit of our minds' (Romans 12.2), so that we can prove that what God wants, true humanity, is best. And so we have to turn, convert, repent, or change our minds, however we might best express it, and 'become like little children'. The tomb has to become the womb. I believe this was the meaning of my own mental picture of regression described earlier. Each person's experience will be different. But Jesus makes it clear that we must all go back to the womb, go 'down into the deep waters', not literally, but symbolically in spirit, and 'be born again' if we are to enjoy the freedom of his, because all of us have been affected by the destructive and divisive propaganda of the Domination System that rules the air waves.

Babies

When preachers speak on such verses, they often focus on the humility of little children (which is rather overplayed judging by the way some of them behave). More appropriate is the thought of complete poverty and helplessness. Babies can do nothing for themselves and have no option but to be entirely trusting and dependent on their parents for everything they need for life. But the best thing about babies is that they are whole. No parent in my experience rejects the bad bits, and accepts the good bits of a new baby. That kind of thinking is absurd. Even though caring for a new-born baby is an exhausting business, a baby brought into the world and accepted by loving parents is accepted as a whole package. Babies can be forgiven *anything*! When they start to be destructive, or express fears, doubts or fantasies, they find acceptance as they own up to them, because there is nothing to hide. A baby surrounded by such secure love does not have to earn acceptance as a reward by working at it, because it cannot do that. A new baby is simply accepted into a loving family as a gift. This is how God treats us. We do not have to achieve *anything* to earn his love. Our status as a child of God is assured

> All who are led by the Spirit of God are children of God. For you did not receive a spirit of slavery to fall back into fear, but you have received a spirit of adoption. When we cry, 'Abba! Father!' it

is that very Spirit bearing witness with our spirit that we are children of God.

(Romans 8.14–16)

God's children

To turn to God and to be born again is to find acceptance, not as a reward which is earned, but as a free gift. We are not 'slaves to the elemental spirits of the world' Domination System (Galatians 4.3), but God's sons and daughters. This is very hard for a world to understand which considers that anything worthwhile has to be worked for. But it is true of our God. He, our heavenly parent, who is both Mother and Father, gives us life and 'being' as his child. He accepts us just as we are, all of us, whole including our doubts, our anxieties and fears, our innate destructiveness, our lusts, our anger, our evil fantasies – all our inner darkness, conscious and unconscious, self-generated or imposed by others on us. There is no need for us to split off any part of our personality, and bury it or project it on some poor relative or colleague, or blame the devil for it. All this that accuses us has been nailed to the cross, and Jesus Christ has conquered the powers that fostered it, that seek to oppress and dominate our world. God in Jesus Christ has entered the chaotic hell of 'non-being' that all this generates, and traps our imprisoned spirit. God in Jesus Christ sets us free to be whole people, and he wants us to remain whole as from day to day we live and move 'in Christ'. As our life progresses we will become aware of all kinds of horrors from the past buried deep within our subconscious or unconscious. But we know that as they are unearthed, we can bring them in complete confidence by confession and prayer to the accepting, merciful and forgiving God to be dealt with and healed. God can accept the dark side of us *because he has been there too*. So we can begin to accept ourselves:

Search me, O God, and know my heart;
test me and know my thoughts.
See if there is any wicked way in me,
and lead me in the way everlasting.

(Psalm 139.23–4)

This is a prayer of integration, of wholeness and of confidence. The waking picture of the warm welcoming open space I referred to in the previous chapter well illustrates this experience of freedom and openness before God.

The place of repentance

Of course there are plenty of sincere Christians who do not speak of this wonderful liberating acceptance of God, probably because they cannot believe it is true themselves. We may well have been told many times that we must repent of our sins and believe in Jesus *as a condition* of being accepted by God. This is to misread the New Testament and make repentance another 'work' that we have to do to earn forgiveness. That is not 'good news' by any stretch of the imagination! When Jesus comes into Galilee and announces the good news of God, he invites people to turn and believe it. The good news is that God is present, near to people in the person of Jesus. Turn and follow him – and forgiveness will follow too.

So we experience forgiveness as we experience God's acceptance through Jesus Christ. Time and time again, Jesus illustrates this point in the Gospel story with all kinds of individuals the religious onlookers count unworthy. It is a constant pain that so much that has been written to help people begin life again with Jesus Christ, makes repentance from sin the entry point of what accepting the gospel means. For example, Nicky Gumbel in his popular booklet, *Why Jesus?*.[7] In the Gospels, 'repent' is usually used without an indirect object and is not qualified by 'sin'. The Gospel begins with God and the announcement of his kingdom. Repentance is our response to his welcoming, accepting and forgiving presence, calling us to turn to him. Good news experience starts when we know we belong to him. Then we can start to learn what believing and turning from sin is all about.[8] Any other way will preserve the work ethic of the system we are supposed to be saved from. This probably explains why so many Christian people still act as though they believe in salvation by 'works', and not by the free grace of God.

The deep in baptism

The sacrament of baptism, the outward, visible sign of this inward experience of new birth, has in the symbolism of the water a remarkable and regular reminder of the *tehom*. We have already noted this in the baptism of Jesus. The Anglican baptism prayer over the water picks this up very fully

> We thank you almighty God, for the gift of water
> to sustain, refresh and cleanse all life.
> Over water the Holy Spirit moved in the
> beginning of creation.
> Through water you led the children of Israel
> from slavery in Egypt to freedom in the promised land.
> In water your Son Jesus received the baptism of John
> and was anointed by the Holy Spirit as the Messiah,
> the Christ,
> to lead us from the death of sin to newness of life.
> We thank you, Father, for the water of baptism.
> In it we are buried with Christ in his death.
> By it we share in his resurrection.
> Through it we are reborn by the Holy Spirit.
> Therefore, in joyful obedience to your Son,
> we baptize into his fellowship those who come
> to him in faith . . .[9]

The significance of these words at an infant baptism is often lost in the hubbub of the occasion. But the symbolism of the *tehom* is all there, the waters of creation, the waters at the Exodus, waters and the Holy Spirit at the baptism of Jesus Christ by John, and being buried with him in his death explored above. In Romans 6 Paul speaks in his own special way of the baptized as *baptized into Christ Jesus*. In other words baptism symbolizes being plunged into Christ's experience of dying and rising as we identify our lives with his. Jesus, as he promised in John 14, is leading us constantly where he is – into the darkness and gloom as well as out of the darkness into the light of glory. So we have here a picture of the tomb and the womb yet again, the picture of a life renewed to begin to live in partnership with him, but not without sharing the pain. Peter similarly links baptism with the Flood imagery in his first letter:

> God waited patiently in the days of Noah, during the building of the ark, in which a few, that is, eight persons, were saved through water. And baptism, which this prefigured, now saves you – not as

> a removal of dirt from the body, but as an appeal to God for a good conscience, through the resurrection of Jesus Christ.
>
> (1 Peter 3.20–1)

Baptism here, as in the Flood before, is not merely a picture of God's salvation through the experience of the deep, but also an instrument of it. Both these pictures imply using lots of water to make the point! The waters of chaos which extinguish life in judgement actually bear up the survivors, becoming their means of salvation. Peter sees the ark containing Noah and his 'family' corresponding to the Church, representing the redeemed human community – one reason why it is important for them to be represented in good numbers at baptism services.

Holding death and life together

It is vitally important we hold these two images together in understanding the Christian faith, suffering and death, and resurrection and new life. We need the symbol of the empty cross, but we also need the symbol of the crucifix too. There is a version of Christianity so full of victory and ecstatic praise that it implies that being risen with Christ and full of the Holy Spirit ought to mean freedom from illness, overflow of spiritual gifts, and near-heavenly experiences of church fellowship! Charismatic renewal is a wonderful blessing for many and has brought a new vitality to worship and ministry in the Church. But it does not give anyone the liberty to be intolerant with those who are very much 'in the depths', suffering pain, depression, trouble and doubt, and who feel remarkably empty of faith and hope. Their experience of Christ can be equally authentic as well. If Christian life is in any way meant to be an *imitatio Christi*, then we are called to journey in *both* aspects of Christ's experience.

> The New Testament presents a living God grappling with the reality of human suffering and spiritual evil, and calling us in the Spirit to enter his death and so share his risen life, each of us living out particular complementary aspects of Christ's life, and all of us, the whole church, making up his risen body, living out the double baptism of cross and resurrection, the double helix of spiritual reality.[10]

A pilgrimage within and yet beyond ourselves

At the beginning of our Christian lives, in the sacrament of baptism, we can have little idea of what living out its significance may entail. This is particularly true if we are baptized as infants. At the font, there is little suffering, except the shock of the water for babies. There are no chaotic stormy waves to face, and immersion, even if it is total, is brief. All that we know, or our parents and friends know, is that God has begun his good work in us. The waters of baptism represent the presence and power of that primeval deep for us. As 'we go through the waters' we are introduced to the task of Christian discipleship for the rest of our lives. We cannot escape them. They remind us that we are not called to an easy ride over the waves during our lifetime.

The Holy Spirit is there too brooding over the waters at every baptism. He is the same Spirit who was mighty wind at creation, who blew back the waters at the crossing of the Red Sea, who descended at the baptism of Jesus in the Jordan, who was present in the agony of the cross, and at the resurrection. He is there to create the being of true humanity out of 'non-being'. This personality of Jesus Christ can be formed in us, as we explore and discover God in the depths of our lives and our circumstances. Christian pilgrimage is thus *an inner journey* into our own depths. We shall find God in the deep there. There will be the darkness of the cross, which may be experienced as a mystical dark night. But the light of the resurrection will be there too bringing liberation to our souls. So God will be there in the deep within us at every stage, exposing and redeeming the darkness, healing and integrating us through the benefits of his cross and calling us to the next adventure of faith.

Christian pilgrimage has *an outer journey* where we transcend ourselves. As we grow closer to our Lord in worship and prayer, we hear his call to mission which draws us out beyond ourselves. This outer journey is about a deeper engagement with the world's darkness, finding the cross in the depths there too. And to bring the world joyful release from the oppressive powers that dominate all of human life, which is all about resurrection.

Chapter 9

Launching Out into the Deep

Exultation is the going
Of an inland soul to sea –
Past the Houses,
Past the Headlands,
Into deep Eternity –
Bred as we, among the mountains,
Can the sailor understand –
That divine intoxication
Of the first league out from land?[1]

It is time to summarize what we have discovered about this elusive concept of the depths and the deep, so real in experience, and yet so difficult to pin down. We have seen how the deep is a timeless theological symbol, not limited by culture or even religious belief. It is what Carl Jung might have described as a living symbol. Jung's living symbols are not just allegories or signs. They are images that actually point to a reality that bridges two worlds, the world of sense and time, and the inner world of spirit. Jung's symbols point to meanings which can never fully be grasped because they are part of God's mysterious activity among his creation. They are seen in our dreams and felt in our bones, rather than remaining definitions or explanations. They fire our imagination and stir our conciousness into emotion and action. The deep is a symbol which is ambivalent in the way it functions. It is not a simple representation of sin or evil. It has enormous potential for good as well. The deep is felt in our human depths, because we are part of the creative process to which it refers, overshadowed and indwelt by the Holy Spirit,

> in hope that the creation itself will be set free from its bondage to decay and will obtain the freedom of the glory of the children of God.
>
> (Romans 8.21)

The chaotic dark empty watery *tehom* at the beginning of the Bible is present as an undercurrent through the revelation of God's purposes, right to the end of the New Testament. We are not told where it came from. Just that it is there, 'theological' raw material for God's use in making a beautiful, ordered world, and developing that magnificent design so that every generation is included throughout the span of time. It represents the 'non-being' which God as creator calls into being. At the same time, the cosmos that God made and is still making is fallen. It still bears God's stamp, and humans still bear his image. But this is veiled because the *tehom* often takes on a personality of its own, resisting the will of God, a *kosmos* or world that is at enmity with its maker through the self-will of its members. The 'uni-verse' God intends thus becomes divided within itself. The darkness which separates night from the light of day becomes a symbol of that rebellion.

In the story of the Flood, in 'Jonah', in the successive destructions of Jerusalem and at many other times in human history, God exercises his sovereignty over the *tehom*, so that it becomes an instrument of his judgement and salvation. This is true both for nations and for individuals. It is humanity, after all, that by rejecting God's ways produces personal, social and environmental chaos. The mythic flood in whatever concrete circumstances it appears simply confirms what humans have done to God's world. In this way rebellion is destroyed by the very instrument that brought it to birth. On other occasions, both in myth and history, God takes on the opposing powers of the deep, most particularly his Son in his incarnation, dying and rising. Whether in judgement or salvation, these movements of the deep serve his ultimate creative purpose. Indeed, at the cross, and in the resurrection, judgement and salvation, we see two sides of one majestic creative event, the decisive conquering of darkness and death, and the triumph of humanity over the forces of chaos.

So the *tehom*, which becomes the hostile *kosmos*, is not simply a mythic concept whose roots lie in ancient spiritual imagination. It has validity for all time. It becomes partly or completely demythologized in national, economic, social and personal systems and forces – cosmic powers which, like the people who inhabit them, can work either for good or ill through the course of history. The sea-monsters which inhabit the deep can be Satan, a Hitler, or a nuclear submarine. The waters of the deep can become the seas, waves and rivers on our world maps. The emptiness of the deep can become the deserts and wide open spaces. The darkness of the deep can become blindness, and death, as well as absence of light. The waters can be experienced metaphorically as well as physically – a ship in a Force 10 gale can do pretty uncomfortable things to our spirits as well as our stomachs! The wilderness can be experienced as barrenness, vulnerability and loneliness. Death and darkness can be experienced as guilt because of sin or depression and paralysing imprisonment of spirit.

The deep and the 'wrath' of God

It is through the operation of this remarkable symbol in Scripture, in history and in experience that we can understand a little more of what the Bible means by the 'anger' of God. Christian history, art and music are full of *Dies Irae* imagery. In this, it seems, God is venting his spleen on wicked people in the most unimaginable torture, horror and violence at the final judgement. This has led to an all-too-common view of God as a capricious and vicious despot who condemns all but a very select few to his thunderbolts now, and to eternal fire and brimstone in the hereafter. This wrath or 'anger' cannot be explained away as a medieval erratic boulder persisting in the outlook of otherwise enlightened Christian people. It does represent something real. It is possible to return to chaos and non-being if we choose the way of hatred rather than love, corruption rather than wholeness, alienation rather than respect and partnership. But when Christians use imagery like this they betray their misunderstanding of apocalyptic symbolism. The disintegration and darkness of hell is always a possibility, but it is something that we choose, never what God wishes to impose on us.

> God did not send the Son into the world to condemn the world, but in order that the world might be saved through him.
>
> (John 3.17)

God is love, and God is good and did not create evil. Yet in the mystery of his creative purposes, and in the process of creation, he has allowed the *tehom*, the darkness which expresses it, and the monsters which inhabit it, to remain until the end of this present age. Fallenness, with the 'knowledge of good and evil', is an essential part of our human consciousness. It tells us all about the power of choice for good or ill. In the end, God can use even evil to serve his good purposes. What cannot be redeemed is consumed in holy fire, to burn as light before his throne. Meanwhile, while the cosmos is moulded through struggle and pain, he can be discovered at work deep in the darkness, as well as gloriously in the light. John Donne expresses this mystery in his own inimitable way:

> The Lord, and only the Lord knows how to wound us, out of love; more than that, to wound us into love, not only with him that wounds us, but into love with the wound itself, with the very affliction that he inflicts upon us. The Lord knows how to strike us so that we shall lay hold upon that hand that strikes us, and kiss the hand that wounds us ... how low so ever God be pleased to cast you, though it be to the earth, yet he does not so much cast you down in doing that, as brings you home.[2]

So the human experiment and the world that goes with it is not inevitably doomed to disaster.

> The risen body of Christ is the seed of the new creation planted within the old chaos. Christ the man is related to the whole cosmos, as is every other human being by an immensely complicated web of genetic, chemical, psychological, intellectual and cultural ties. But this part of the cosmos, the part which is Christ's manhood is risen and glorified. The shock-waves go through the whole; every part is affected. His risen body is like a radio-active substance lodged in the heart of the universe.[3]

By entering and redeeming the *tehom*, Jesus Christ has entered into our alienated human condition and transformed it. He has decisively conquered the chaotic god-like power of the forces of the deep, without overriding the freedom men and women have to choose the way of humanity or not. He is master of the depths. He walks on water. And he still treats us like responsible creatures. We can still choose the terrifying, meaningless, heartless way of 'anger'. We can return the earth to the 'non-being' of chaos by consistently refusing to listen. Like Jesus, we still have to face the forces of the deep for there is still much to be brought to birth in God's mysterious plan. So he urges us not to be overcome by the powers of the deep which remain as long as time, which itself is one of the chief powers, but to turn around to him, to experience the wind of his creative, redeeming Spirit who will make us part of his new creation. To hear his call, to respond to his voice, to live 'in him' and not 'in' any oppressive rival, and continue the fight to establish God's 'kingdom on earth as it is in heaven'. He calls us to be nothing less than his partners in the redemptive process, so that everything, even history itself with its destructive power struggles, can be united in him,

> according to his good pleasure that he set forth in Christ, as a plan for the fullness of time, to gather up all things in him, things in heaven and things on earth.
>
> (Ephesians 1.9–10)

This partnership is nothing less than the agenda for the Church's mission.

Manipulation and control: the alternative to spiritual growth

There has never been a moment when Western people have found faith which leads to Christian discipleship within the Church so hard. This is not because they are less spiritual than previous generations. Far from it, we have seen that beneath the superficial materialism of Western civilization there is a deep spiritual search for truth and meaning to life. This search is highlighted in the multitude of faiths and philosophies on offer, each making their own truth-claims.

The task of the Church is to appeal to a millennial generation hooked on the idea of control in this spiritual supermarket. And control is the exact opposite of the challenge the deep presents to people. Today, everyone wants control of their lives, their health, their environment, so that they can get what they want where they want it at a moment's notice. Control is the selling point behind most advertisements. Control is built into human expectations after three centuries of unprecedented advances in science and technology. Control is at the heart of most party political programmes and media spin-doctoring. Control is behind the spectacular growth of the Internet, giving the power to produce information about anything required from anywhere in the world at our fingertips. Control is an individual way of pursuing the accepted Western ethos of personal achievement and domination. 'We are part of a culture that holds together consumer satiation and petty obedience. That tight alliance serves to keep us as the agenda, an excuse for not ceding life beyond self, an inability to transfer attention beyond our needs and appetites.'[4] So which God shall we choose from the many on offer? It is natural for us, if we believe there is a God, that he (she) should be an extension of the godlike powers already at our disposal, and many today think and do what comes as second nature because it is inbred into them by culture and expectations.

It is hard to have to reckon with the God of the depths who refuses to be manipulated by anything or anybody. 'God is not ours to possess, but we are His or Hers to be possessed by.'[5] This God is as much of a problem for the believer as for the unbeliever, because believers are not immune from false impressions once they take a step of faith. Because of our frail, fallen condition, it is his mercy that makes Jesus Christ, T. S. Eliot's 'tiger' appear as

> the word within a word, unable to speak a word, swaddled in darkness.[6]

Time and again it is the 'righteous' who get God wrong, as much as the sinners. It is they after all who hounded and crucified Jesus Christ – not the poor, the outcast, and the unbelievers! The doctrine of the God of the deep confounds triviality – and religious pride. The constant presence of the deep is terribly humbling. It reminds us, even if we think we understand God's ways, that we often inhabit dark places in our 'certainties'. Believers too live in the shadows formed by the playing of the heavenly light on the ceaseless waves which form the patterns and pressures of people and circumstances upon us. If we embrace faith for protection against real life, and many do, we need to examine what we're hiding behind. What we believe is protecting us, may in fact be shielding us from the truth. Maybe we too are guilty of the sin of Adam when God called him in the garden. To live in the light would make us too exposed, too vulnerable . . .

> This is the judgement, that the light has come into the world, and people loved darkness rather than light because their deeds were evil.
>
> (John 3.19)

The modern demand for a nurturing, predictable God who answers every human need without question is a vindication of the truth of the parable of the Fall. It is a sign that deep within the human psyche there is an image of what life in relationship with God could be like – and also what, existentially, the whole cosmos has fallen from. But even the images of existentially 'remembered' truth have been distorted by the deep through the effects of the Fall, rather like the image of a person's face above water is distorted to a viewer looking at it from below the water level. We want that relationship on our terms – infantile consumers in God's world, rather than grown-up partners with him in the business of creation and re-creation, to bring his kingdom to challenge the rebellion and distortion of the institutions and powers which make up the *kosmos*. We need to grow up.

Meeting God in the deep

The place of life-changing possibilities

The solution to life's problems and disappointments is not a conjuring trick produced out of the blue by some indulgent deity. It is a new awareness and awakening within *our own inner depths*: facing uncomfortable buried facts, changing our attitudes, seeking forgiveness, accepting challenges, which can all lead to a growth in personality because we meet God *there* like 'Jonah' of old, and not on some fictitious silvery cloud high above our murky condition. In a familiar scene in Luke's Gospel, Jesus invites his disciples to launch out into the deep to grow mature in partnership with him.

> He sat down and taught the crowds from the boat. When he had finished speaking, he said to Simon, 'Put out into the deep water and let down your nets for a catch.' Simon answered, 'Master, we have worked all night long, but have caught nothing. Yet if you say so, I will let down the nets.' When they had done this, they caught so many fish that their nets were beginning to break ... Then Jesus said to Simon, 'Do not be afraid; from now on you will be catching people.' When they had brought their boats to shore, they left everything and followed him.
>
> (Luke 5.3–6,10–11)

For Simon Peter and all who would be Christ's disciples and grow towards humanity, the deep is not only a symbol of evil, or of the inevitable judgement which follows from consistently and deliberately ignoring God's way. The deep is a place of God's possibilities. Jesus Christ calls his disciples from the relative comfort of the familiar sights, sounds and smells of the fishing business to a risky, life-changing adventure, which means a change of priorities and direction ('from now on . . .'). So it becomes a place where hearing and acting on Christ's call can mean a new beginning in life, and lead to a creative partnership with him.

The deep that day was like the river in Robert de Board's psychological adventure based on *The Wind in the Willows*: 'Only the river moved on, black and sinuous, always changing, yet always the same, creating a boundary for some animals, a highway for others, and with a suppressed energy and power that was only dangerous when ignored.'[7] If we want to grow up, we need to jump in the water and move with the flow. The waters of the deep are a barrier for some of us. We sense it is a place of danger because the latent possibilities of good and evil are there. It does represent the unknown because it is the place of faith. But for would-be disciples, it is where God is, and where the next challenge is; it is where we ought to be, out there in the water rather than shivering on the bank. Jesus makes the same point in the parable of the talents.

There is no future in burying what we are given, especially if what we are given is life itself, because we are afraid and it seems the safest thing to do (Matthew 25.14–30/Luke 19.11–27). The presence of the deep invites faith and participation throughout our lives, for there we shall grow to be our true selves.

The place of rescue and renewal

The whole Bible is the story of rescue and renewal of faith, hope and life itself. Often, God's people find themselves overcome by the adventure of the deep, because they have made the wrong choices, turned in the wrong direction, or thought they could save themselves. The deep may threaten their progress in the form of stormy waters, howling wilderness, or the peril of death itself. Psalm 107 celebrates God's deliverance through these depths, whether wandering in desert wastes (vv. 4–9), sitting in the darkness and gloom of a self-made prison (vv. 10–16), or tossed around by the raging waters in the struggle to run a business (vv. 23–32). With each deliverance comes the refrain

> O give thanks to the Lord, for he is good;
> for his steadfast love endures for ever.

This is a reminder that in the course of a lifetime, in the creation of our mature humanity, we make many mistakes. We experience both the faith possibilities and the threats of the deep through success and failure. The heavenly potter who is still working the clay of the cosmos in his hands is endlessly compassionate, much more ready to forgive us than we are ourselves. He rescues us again and again, as Jesus did for Peter who had denied him before the cross, back again on the seashore.

> When they had finished breakfast, Jesus said to Simon Peter, 'Simon son of John, do you love me more than these?' He said to him,'Yes, Lord; you know that I love you.' Jesus said to him,'Feed my lambs.'
>
> (John 21.15)

The Bible never whitewashes its heroes. They are human beings like us. We can learn from incidents like this in the Gospel story. And God's creative purposes are advanced as we are prepared to take risks and reach out beyond ourselves to where he is leading us.

The place of revelation and discovery

It is only when we engage with God in the depths that we discover who we really are and what human life is about. The Israelites were a rabble of slaves until they discovered they could be a nation through the experience of privations and mistakes in the wilderness. Jesus could only discover what kind of Messiah he was to be through the fearful experience of testing in the desert. The apostles could only discover who they were through sharing the loneliness, the misunderstanding and ultimately the cross of Jesus Christ as they journeyed with him. So it will be with us. The deep is the place where we discover ourselves; where we are stripped of all pretensions, and the God we reach out to is stripped of our unwarranted assumptions and projections. We can endlessly speculate on the edge of the shore, but we only really discover the truth when we trust ourselves to the waves. The people of Israel were able to reflect and write about the God of the deep who redeems as he creates and re-creates through their pilgrimage experience of desert and exile. The Pharisee Saul discovered who Jesus was after being blinded by the radiance of his vision on the road to Damascus. That experience and the voice he heard coloured his theological thinking and changed the direction of his mission in life. There is a place for affirming creeds. But belief-systems only really start to live in the heart after taking the plunge of faith. That is what baptism is all about!

The deep and the Church's mission agenda

If we think of the experience of the depths simply as 'my problem' we are in danger of falling into the modern trap of examining, finding and recovering faith purely in individualistic terms. We are never called to confront the waters for any length of time on our own. For the Bible, the opposite of chaos is community. The Gospels picture the Church as an ark, with Christ in the stern where the rudder is, in stormy weather and in calm seas. In the boat, his disciples are not insulated from the wind and the waves of the deep, but are called to face them together with him. The Gospels also picture the Church as a community founded on the faith of Peter and the apostles – a Rock which can withstand the power of the wind and the waves, no matter what the opposition may fling against it. Throughout church history, these images have often been misunderstood and distorted by the faithful:

> In 1523, the then Pope, Adrian V, a Dutchman, had been presented with a picture called 'The Barque of Peter' by a Florentine painter. The painting showed the ship raised above the sea by angels blowing eschatological trumpets. Immediately beneath the ship the sea was calm, but all around were angry waves. On the top deck sat the Pope with his papal guard around him. The sails were limp, but the papal flag fluttered above them. Out of the little portholes peeped the people of God gazing at the arms, legs and heads of drowning heretics, schismatics and sinners. Around the rudder of the raised ship was a cluster of angels reading an illuminated text, 'Thou art Peter, and upon this rock I shall build my Church.' Pope Adrian was horrified at the gift, saying that this was not his ship. He wanted the ship to be on the waters, the sails filled, and he wanted to be saved along with all the heretics, schismatics and sinners. Shortly afterwards the Pope died. Some said he had been poisoned.[8]

Not everyone today has the wisdom or big-hearted compassion of that particular Pope. The temptation for the Church in history has been to be exclusive and triumphalistic, especially when, as at present in Western society, it is in danger of being ignored.

Where then should the Church be in relation to the deep? Figures 3, 4 and 5 illustrate three possibilities:

1 The Church as an island

Island churches are consciously or unwittingly separate from their surroundings. They vary from harmless holy huddles, religious relics of the culture of a bygone age, to coercive and dangerously exclusive sectarian communities which impose fearful control over their members. Island churches have a typically dualistic faith, where the dark world beyond their doors is firmly seen to be under the control of the devil beyond the deep water of sin and evil. By contrast, these people claim to live in the light, and mark their identity by distinctive teaching, patterns of worship and lifestyle. Most are not really interested in sharing the faith, except on their terms. Tight membership rules and expectations, and black-and-white literalistic doctrines, make joining very unattractive to all but the most determined. They feel safe, anticipating heaven within the confines of their worship, which becomes a kind of drug. The right kind of preaching, hymns, songs and techniques for prayer are popped like hallucinogenic pills. The 'grace' of God, which they claim has saved them out of the world, is experienced as the security of knowing that they are among the elect, and everyone else is wrong and doomed to hell.

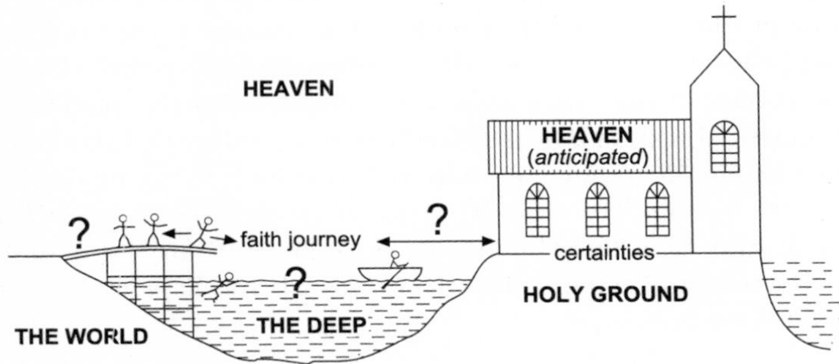

Figure 3 The Church as an island

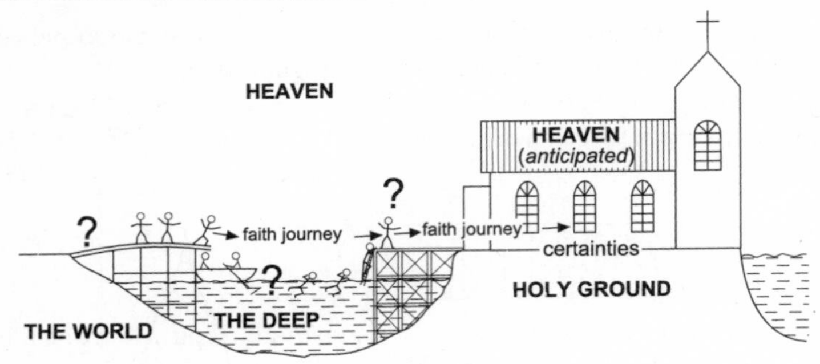

Figure 4 The Church as a pier

2 The Church as a pier

Most traditional Christian congregations have rightly rejected such a restricted view of church. They really believe that Jesus Christ has come to transform the world, not just themselves. They want to get in touch with the community around, and they have set about building a pier out into the deep whose length depends on their vision and spiritual generosity. This makes it possible for intrepid and persistent seekers who really want to discover God's love to reach the rope ladders hung out from the pier, like ALPHA groups, and baptism policies. They are sincere and resourceful in their practice of faith, but they talk about 'outreach' (which often means in-drag), and 'claiming the world for Christ' as though he cannot be present anywhere unless *they* do the work.

But they are hampered, first, by the implicit dualism of their teaching: they talk with conviction about the 'secular world' as though the Church is on holier ground than the rest; faith is rather self-conscious; salvation is privatized; heaven is very much for the future, and we have to be saved *from* the wicked world with its waves and breakers of doubt, by spiritual certainties. And second, they are hampered by an inability to speak clearly to the culture they are trying to address. Salvation and membership are still very much on their terms. Enquirers still have to believe before they can belong. Some disciples are made and rejoice, but many who seek cannot find handholds in their searching and easily get discouraged.

3 The Church as a bridge

This kind of church imitates Jesus Christ in his incarnation, whose

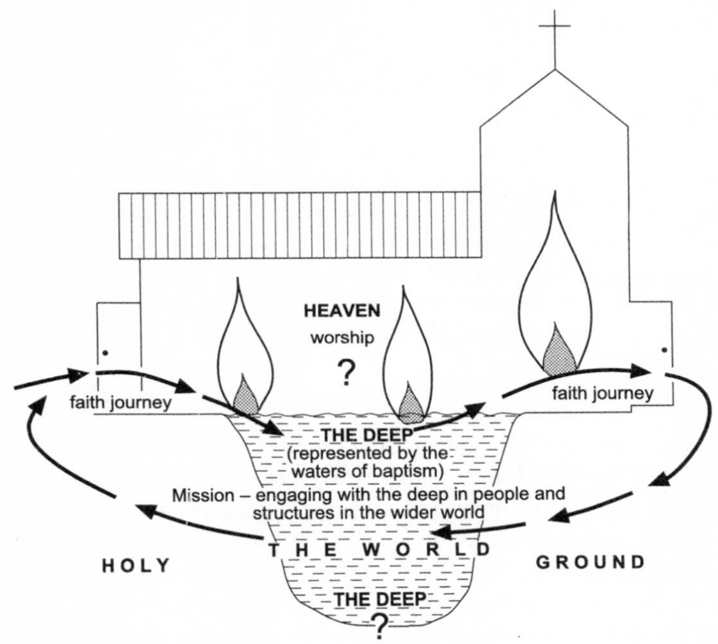

Figure 5 The Church as a bridge (using the ancient 3-decker universe as an imaginative model)

body it represents. It is prepared to take risks. It *recognizes* that God is at work in the community and blesses the whole neighbourhood with its presence and embodiment of distinctive Christian faith and values. It *equips* its members to be part of the community, and values people and institutions which do not necessarily have a Christian label. It *welcomes* the surprises of the Holy Spirit, being open to God, and to every kind of person he sends. It will also welcome opportunities to share faith naturally, building bridges by acknowledging the natural spirituality even of those who do not claim to be believers. It *offers* attractive church buildings which are open every day, where anyone searching for a holy place can be reminded of the God who opens his heart to them. The building, as well as the congregation, will therefore be a sacrament of presence.

Such churches will model belonging before believing. They will have fuzzy edges with a large fringe of people 'just tasting'. Doorways into the fellowship will be scattered all over the community in cells and groups as well as within voluntary community organizations and schools. These cells will provide half-way houses and stepping-stone groups for people to take the steps leading to mature discipleship, recognizing the long journey many people have to make without any kind of faith background. This church will provide a spacious place to explore faith and feelings, fascinating enquirers with the story of God. It will be a safe place for people to belong, and to work through their struggles to believe, among friends who are unshockable, and give them time to respond.

Embracing the depths

It would be easy to portray such congregations as soft-centred, so little different from their surroundings that they cut no ice in their witness. So what safeguards are there to maintain distinctive faith without standing out like a sore thumb? The key is that the bridge church is willing to embrace the deep and to encourage people to face the waters at each stage of their lives. First, the waters in the adventure of faith, exploring discipleship with sensitivity and conviction leading to their representation in baptism. But the font, or the baptismal pool, is not an end in itself. It points to eucharistic worship – another representation of the waters, this time in the mystery of faith and fellowship with God. Too many churches today are frightened of this aspect of the deep, preferring oversimplified 'McDonaldized' worship which has an answer for everything and is devoid of beauty and mystery, leaving worshippers short-changed and unsatisfied.[9] Worship which embodies the deep makes space for that sense of wonder and awe which is in such short supply. It means worship which is truly sacramental, involving drama, art, music and silence; worship as theophany which is itself converting involving all the senses; worship that converts, not just to Jesus Christ, but to the world around where he is at work.

Jesus once said, 'you will know them by their fruits' (Matthew 7.20). In doing so, he looks back to the fruitful earth of Genesis 1, and forward to the renewed heaven and earth where each member is joyfully fruitful under the movement of God's Spirit. The real test of a congregation is not only whether it brings people to committed discipleship through baptism. Nor simply whether the experience of church means a real encounter with the living God in worship. But whether its members are braving the third great aspect of the deep as well: revealing God's kingdom in society, in their everyday witness: in dialogue, in service, and in compassion, challenging the 'systems' of the *kosmos* which oppress, and the attitudes that marginalize. This is the witness that illustrates Christ in the community, attracting, puzzling and sometimes forcing onlookers to take sides, just as Jesus of Nazareth did in Galilee and Judaea in the Gospel story. This is that unmistakeable Christian witness which changes people and situations for the better: risky, costly and sacrificial, confronting the darkness and releasing the captives.

For the Church is a partner with the Spirit in the re-creation of the earth through the victory of Jesus over the powers of the deep. We are called to declare that peace which touches the hearts of humankind, the structures of society and the cosmos itself; that peace which marks his kingdom, as Jesus did to the wind and the waves on the boat on the Sea of Galilee.

> He said to them, 'Why are you afraid? Have you still no faith?' And they were filled with great awe and said to one another, 'Who then is this, that even the wind and the sea obey him?'
>
> (Mark 4.40–1)

As we do, we are called to grow up in faith not by embracing 'certainties', but by embracing the deep by living with all its doubts and mystery. For the deep is where we shall find God at work. And to walk with, to live with, and to worship and serve Jesus Christ, is not so much to be provided with a set of convenient 'answers', but to have him raise endless questions which lead to the next steps of faith and action together until one day we join the band of the conquerors by the 'sea of glass mixed with fire', singing the song of Moses and the song of the Lamb.

> Great and amazing are your deeds,
> Lord God the Almighty!
> Just and true are your ways,
> King of the nations!
> Lord, who will not fear

and glorify your name?
For you alone are holy.
All nations will come
and worship before you,
for your judgements have been revealed.

(Revelation 15.3–4)

NOTES

Preface

1 Gerard Hughes, *God of Surprises*, Darton, Longman & Todd, 1987, pp. 34–5.

1 Estonia: Faith after the Soviet deluge

1 Details taken from *Official Report of the Joint Accident Investigation Committee* from Estonia, Finland and Sweden (Helsinki, 1997); and Denise Albrighton, 'Group sifts through mysterious *Estonia* Disaster', *Baltic Times*, Tallinn, 10–16 September, 1998.

2 Toomas Paul, statistics from *Situation of the Lutheran Church of Estonia during the Soviet Period and the Process of Becoming Independent.* Text of lecture given to the Eleventh Anglo-Scandinavian Pastoral Conference, Tallinn, 24 May 1996.

3 Paul, *Situation of the Lutheran Church*, p. 3.

4 Lorna and Michael Bourdeaux, *Ten Growing Soviet Churches*, Marc Europe,1987, pp. 23–4.

5 Michael Bourdeaux, *Gorbachev, Glasnost and the Gospel*, Hodder & Stoughton, 1990, pp. 148–52.

6 Paul, *Situation of the Lutheran Church*, p. 2.

7 Gustav Kutsar, sermon delivered on a visit to US Lutheran churches, 25 May 1998.

8 Lorna and Michael Bourdeaux, *Soviet Churches*, pp. 25–31.

9 Translated from the Estonian by Eero Vihman. Sleeve notes, Veljo Tormis, *Epic Fields*, FD0030/2, Forte Record Company, Tallinn, 1995.

10 Sleeve notes, Urmas Sisask, *Eesti Missa*, Estonian Radio Recording, 1998.

11 See Lorna and Michael Bourdeaux, *Soviet Churches*, pp. 43–58.

12 Mircea Eliade, *Myths, Dreams and Mysteries*, Harvill Press, 1966, pp. 124–6.
13 Jaan Kaplinski, *Through the Forest*, Harvill Press, 1996, p. 20.

2 *The power of the sea*

1 Jaan Kaplinski, *Through the Forest*, Harvill Press, 1996, p. 58.
2 Mircea Eliade, *Patterns in Comparative Religion*, London, 1958, pp. 188–9.
3 Kaplinski, *Through the Forest*, p. 58.
4 English translation of J. W. von Goethe, *Rinaldo*, set to music by Brahms as his Opus 50.
5 Joseph Conrad, *The Mirror of the Sea*, Oxford University Press, 1988 edn, p. 31.
6 Marie O'Brien, 'Atlantic Drive' in Ian Walton (ed.), *Poetry Now 1992 Northern Ireland*, p. 64.
7 Joseph Conrad, *The Heart of Darkness*, Penguin, 1994 edn, p. 12.
8 Conrad, *Mirror of the Sea*, pp. 136–7.
9 See Per Pettersson, *Implicit Religion Turned Explicit: A Case History of the Estonia disaster*. Paper presented at the 19th Denton Conference on Implicit Religion, 10–12 May 1996, University of Karlstad Service Research Center.
10 Pettersson, *Implicit Religion*, p. 26.
11 Unattributed, in Pettersson, ibid., p. 30.
12 Per Ragnar, in Pettersson, ibid.
13 I owe this perceptive insight to Dr Anne Richards.
14 Carl Jung, *Modern Man in Search of a Soul*, Ark edn, 1984.
15 English translation of Friedrich Hölderlin, *Hyperions Schicksalslied*, set to music by Brahms as his Opus 54.

3 *Charting the ways of the deep*

1 William Cowper (1731–1800).
2 The literature here is vast. '*Tohu* is used elsewhere to mean in physical terms a trackless waste (Deuteronomy 32.10; Job 6.18), emptiness (Job 26.7), chaos (Isaiah 24.10; 34.11; 45.18) and metaphorically what is baseless or futile (1 Samuel 12.21; Isaiah 29.21)' (D. Kidner, *Genesis*, Tyndale, 1968, p. 44). *Tehom* has a clear linguistic kinship with *Tiamat*, the personified ocean of the

Babylonian creation myth. For excellent concise overviews, see Gerhard von Rad, *Genesis*, SCM, 1963, pp. 45–9, who sees *tohu wa-bohu* and *tehom* as 'an intermediate state between nothingness and creation', and Claus Westermann, *Creation*, SPCK, 1971.

3 Joseph Conrad, *The Mirror of the Sea*, Oxford University Press, 1988 edn, p. 71.

4 Rosemary Hughes, *Haydn*, Master Musicians Series, Dent, 1950, p. 114.

5 George A. F. Knight, *Theology in Pictures*, Edinburgh, 1981, p. 15.

6 Jaan Kaplinski, *The Same Sea in Us All*, Harvill Press, 1990, p. 32.

7 Knight, *Theology in Pictures*, pp. 73–4.

8 von Rad, *Genesis*, p. 124.

9 Walter Brueggemann, *Biblical Perspectives on Evangelism*, Abingdon Press, 1993, pp. 7–47 develops this three-decker universe theme attractively to illuminate the false dichotomy often posed between evangelism and social action.

10 Westermann, *Creation*, pp. 17–31.

11 Jeremiah 4.23–9 pictures the anticipated desolation of Palestine as a return to the pre-creation *tohu wa-bohu*. The desert was and is always a threat to the establishment and survival of ordered civilization in the Near East.

12 George A. F. Knight, *Ruth and Jonah*, rev. edn, SCM, 1966, pp. 56–87, is a brief but unsurpassed commentary on the message and place of Jonah in Old and New Testaments.

13 'Height nor depth' here may have an astronomical origin, apparently referring to the top and bottom of the pillars supporting the firmament of heaven. This thought parallels Psalm 139.8–9 about the all-embracing presence of God, even where he is most felt to be absent (see 1 Enoch 18.3, 11 and Walter Wink, *Naming the Powers*, Fortress, 1982, pp. 49–50).

4 The deep in the journey of life

1 Gerard Manley Hopkins, 'The Wreck of the Deutschland', 65–72, in *Selected Poetry*, Oxford University Press, 1996, p. 100.

2 For the place of tears in mystic spirituality see George A. Maloney, *Inward Stillness*, Dimension Books, 1976, pp. 105–19.

3 Kosuke Koyama, *Three-Mile-an-Hour God*, SCM, 1979, p. 4.

4 Ibid., p. 7.

5 T. S. Eliot, *Choruses from the Rock*, I, in *Collected Poems*, Faber, 1963, p. 163.
6 Ibid., VII, p. 176.
7 Walter Brueggemann, *Praying the Psalms*, St Mary's Press, 1993, p. 24.
8 and 9 Ibid., p. 37.

5 The Church: bridge over troubled waters?

1 T. S. Eliot, *Choruses from the Rock*, X, in *Collected Poems*, Faber, 1963, p. 183.
2 Paul Tillich, *Shaking of the Foundations*, SCM, 1949, pp. 1–11.
3 Per Pettersson, *Implicit Religion Turned Explicit: A Case History of the Estonia Disaster*. Paper presented at the 19th Denton Conference on Implicit Religion, 10–12 May 1996, University of Karlstad Service Research Center, p. 15.
4 English translation of F. Hölderlin, *Schicksalslied*, from Brahms, Opus 54.
5 Henry F. Lyte (1783–1847).
6 David Hay and Rebecca Nye, *The Spirit of the Child*, Fount, 1998, p. 21.
7 Pettersson, *Implicit Religion*, p. 5.
8 Walter Wink, *Engaging the Powers*, Fortress, 1993, p. 51. For Wink's splendid exposé of the 'Denomination System' outlined in these paragraphs, see further pp. 51–85; also Alan Richardson, *An Introduction to the Theology of the New Testament*, SCM, 1958, pp. 211–14.

6 Monsters of the deep

1 John Milton, *Paradise Lost*, Book II, 795–7.
2 Iris Murdoch, *The Sea, the Sea*, Faber, 1978.
3 Walter Wink, *Unmasking the Powers*, Fortress, 1986, pp. 9–50, to which this chapter is greatly indebted.
4 Ibid., p. 18.
5 Ibid., p. 24.
6 George A. F. Knight, *Theology in Pictures*, Edinburgh, 1981, p. 37.
7 Adapted from Wink, *Unmasking the Powers*, p. 32.
8 In Wink, ibid., p. 45. Wink's thinking on the psychopathology of

Legion and his community follows René Girard, *Violence and the Sacred*, Johns Hopkins University Press, 1985.

9 Wink, *Unmasking the Powers*, p. 46.

10 Ibid., p. 40.

7 Redeeming the deep

1 Walter Wink, *Engaging the Powers*, Fortress, 1993, pp. 59–63.

2 N. T. Wright, *Jesus and the Victory of God*, SPCK, 1996, p. 605.

3 George A. F. Knight, *Ruth and Jonah*, rev. edn, SCM, 1966, pp. 78–81.

4 St John Damascene, *c.* 750 CE.

5 Kenneth Grayston, 'The Darkness of the Cosmic Sea', *Theology*, April 1952, pp. 123–7.

6 G. M. Hopkins, 'O Death, Death', in *Selected Poetry*, Oxford University Press, 1996, p. 61.

7 C. S. Lewis, *The Great Divorce*, Fontana, 1972.

8 Alan Richardson, *Introduction to the Theology of the New Testament*, SCM, 1958, pp. 210–11, has an excellent summary of the arguments over this disputed passage, including E. G. Selwyn's masterly analysis, which contrasts rather than combines 1 Peter 3.19 and 4.6 (*1 Peter*, Macmillan, 1946, pp. 197–201 and 314–62).

9 Samuel Crossman (1624–83).

10 Jürgen Moltmann, *Jesus Christ for Today's World*, SCM, 1994, p. 31.

11 Ibid., p. 36.

12 Timothy Rees (1874–1939).

13 Moltmann, *Jesus Christ*, p. 42.

8 The tomb and the womb of the deep

1 Charles Wesley (1707–88).

2 Richard Burridge, *Four Gospels, One Jesus?*, SPCK, 1994, p. 133.

3 Titus 3.5 (of individuals) and Matthew 19.28 (of the cosmos), but see the similar *kaine ktisis* (2 Corinthians 5.17; Galatians 6.15).

4 Frank Lake, *Clinical Theology*, Darton, Longman & Todd, 1966, pp. 134–6.

5 See also Leslie Virgo (ed.), *First Aid in Pastoral Care*, T & T Clark, 1987, pp. 24–7.

6 Suggested by the imagery of Ephesians 4.14 and James 1.5–8.
7 Nicky Gumbel, *Why Jesus?*, Kingsway, 1991, p. 19.
8 So Peter in Luke 5.8.
9 Common Worship, *Initiation*, Church House Publishing, 1998, pp. 23–4.
10 Philip Seddon, *Darkness*, Grove Spirituality Series No. 5, 1982, p. 6.

9 Launching out into the deep

1 Ted Hughes, *A Choice of Emily Dickinson's Verse*, Faber, 1968, p. 17.
2 John Donne, *From a sermon preached at St Paul's*, Sunday after the Conversion of St Paul, 1625.
3 Maria Boulding, *The Coming of God*, SPCK, 1982, pp. 154–5.
4 Walter Brueggemann, *The Psalms and the Life of Faith*, Fortress, 1995, p. 263.
5 M. Scott Peck, *Further along the Road Less Travelled*, Simon & Schuster, 1993, p. 166.
6 T. S. Eliot, 'Gerontion', in *Collected Poems*, Faber, 1963, p. 39.
7 Robert de Board, *Counselling for Toads*, Routledge, 1998, p. 1.
8 Gerard Hughes, *God Where Are You?*, Darton, Longman & Todd, p. 110.
9 John Drane, *Faith in a Changing Culture*, Marshall Pickering, 1997, pp. 110–15.

Index

Acts of the Apostles: Paul's shipwreck 43
Adrian V, Pope 126
Ainger, Arthur 16
alcohol 74
ALPHA groups 128
Angel of the North (sculpture) 74
anothen 103

Babylonia 36, 38:
  creation myth 31
  water myth 17
baptism 113–15, 116, 130
Biblical images and stories:
  barren desert 48–52
  creation 29, 31–2, 38
  exile and Exodus 35–9, 49, 92–3
  the Flood 33–5
  Jonah 39–40
  Moses in the water 39
  opposing powers of the deep 118
  the perception of the universe 32
  Satan 76–7
  see also Jewish people
Bildt, Carl 25
birth:
  creation and labour 103–4
  Nicodemus's question 102–3
  re-birth 104–5
  womb and tomb 104
Board, Robert de 124
Bourdeaux, Lorna and Michael 10
Brahms, Johannes 18: *Song of Destiny* 60
Brueggemann, Walter: *Praying the Psalms* 55–6
Brunner, Emil 106
Burridge, Richard: *Four Gospels, One Jesus?* 102

Cameron, James 26–7
churches:
  as bridges 128–30
  contemporary attitudes 58–60
  disillusionment and loss of faith 65–6
  expectations of control 121–3
  fellowship 63
  fundamentalism 63–5
  as islands 127
  kosmos 70–1
  Millennium celebrations 66–7
  mission agenda 126–30
  as piers 127
cinema: portrayal of mysterious sea 22
Clinical Theology movement 54
Colossians, Letter to: authority and power 89–90
Conrad, Joseph 19–20

Conrad, Joseph (*cont.*)
  Heart of Darkness 23
  The Mirror of the Sea 30
control: modern expectations 121–3
Corinthians, First Letter to: physical and spiritual body 88
creation:
  Babylonian 31
  baptism of Jesus 91
  birth as 103–4, 117
  Genesis 29, 31–2
  Haydn's interpretation 31
  Psalms 38
  the seas 29
cross image: Estonian representations 13–14

Darwin, Charles:
  Origin of Species 27
  reaction against 63
Debussy, Claude: *La Mer* 19
deep darkness:
  depression 54–7
  power of God 53–4
desert:
  journey of barrenness to fruitfulness 48–52
  temptation of Jesus 78–9, 125
Deuteronomy, Book of: Hebrew *tehom* 30
Domination System 68–71, 108
Donne, John 120
Dvořák, Antonin 18–19

education 66, 67
El Niño effect 22
Elgar, Sir Edward 27
Eliade, Mircea 12:
  water imagery 16–17
Eliot, T. S. 122
Ephesians, Letter to 69, 121
Estonia:
  Christian family life 11–12
  churches maintain faith 4–7, 9–10, 14
  history and Soviet control 2–4, 70
  music 7–9
  national spirit as angel 74
  nature 12–13
  sinking of the ferry 1–2
Estonia (ferry):
  effect in Sweden 24–5
  sinking 1–2
evil:
  dualism of heaven and earth 60
  God's protection from 81
  see also Satan
Exodus, Book of 37–8, 92–3:
  Moses in the water 39

family: maintaining faith 11–12
flesh 87–8
The Flood 33–5, 118:
  and baptism 91, 114–15
  symbolism within the Gospel 42

Gehenna 52, 95
Genesis, Book of:
  creation 29, 32
  the Flood 34
  good and evil 81
Gerasene demons 82–4
Girard, René 83–4
Gnosticism 60–1, 64–5

God:
  abandonment of Jesus 99–101
  dualism of heaven and earth 60
  in human tragedies 28
  as Lord of Darkness 75–6
  sovereignty over *tehom* 118–19
  'wrath' 119–21
Goethe, Johann Wolfgang von: *Rinaldo* 18
Gormley, Antony: *Angel of the North* 74
Gumbel, Nicky: *Why Jesus?* 113

Hagström, Annika: *Like a Bridge Over Troubled Waters* 59
Hay, David 67
Haydn, Franz Josef: *The Creation* 31
heaven and earth:
  Domination System 70
  the Fall 96
  popular dualism 59–63
hell 95–8
Hokusai, Katsushika 19
Hölderlin, Friedrich 62
Hopkins, Gerard Manley 95
Hosea, Book of 98–9
human beings:
  babies and children 111–13
  burying the bad for the look of success 109–10
  cycle of relationships 107–9
  good and evil 81
  inner and outer journey 116
  life and death 115
  life-changing forces 44–5
  likeness to God 51–2
  repentance 113
  true conversion 110–11

Isaiah, Book of 1:
  exile 36–7
  renewal in water 46
  sea image 39
  vision and insight 53–4

James, Letter of: the devil 77
Jesus Christ:
  baptism 90–3, 114
  crucifixion and descent into hell 92–3, 94–8
  cry of the God-forsaken 92, 99–101
  cycle of relationships 105–7
  endurance of hellish places 93–4
  fishing with disciples 123–4
  Jesus and the depths 41–3, 71
  master of the depths 120–1
  meaning of the crucifixion 98–100
  ministers to others in hell 94
  puzzles Nicodemus 102–3
  redemption 87
  temptation 78–9
Jewish people: exile and Exodus 35–9, 49, 92–3
Job, Book of:
  birth 103–4
  desert experience 48
  testing by Satan 76–7
John, Gospel of 41:
  darkness over light 122
  Jesus and Simon Peter 125
  kosmos 68–9, 70
  Nicodemus is puzzled 102–3
  saving the world 119

John the Prophet *see* Revelation, Book of
Jonah, Book of 39–40, 91
Jung, Carl 117
  Modern Man in Search of a Soul 27–8
  spiritual life 75

Kalevala (epic poem) 9
Kaplinski, Jaan 9, 12: water imagery 17
Kapp, Artur 7
Karl Gustav, King of Sweden 25
kosmos 68–9, 118: Domination System 68–71
Koyama, Kosuke 49–50
Kutsar, Gustav 5
Kuum, Alexander 6

Lake, Frank 54, 106
Lewis, C. S.: *The Great Divorce* 95
Lonnebo, Bishop Martin 25
Luke, Gospel of:
  Jesus fishing with disciples 123
  Jesus's baptism 92
  roaring of the sea 42
  Satan as tester 77
  waiting for the Holy Spirit 50–1
Lutheran Church: in Estonia 3, 4–5, 10

Mark, Gospel of:
  crucifixion 92
  having faith over the deep 131
  Jesus and the sea 41
  Jesus's baptism 92
material world: spirits of 73–5
Matthew, Gospel of:
  symbolism of the Flood 42
Methodist Church: in Estonia 5–7
Moltmann, Jürgen: *The Crucified God* 98–100
monsters of the deep:
  in Revelation 84–6
  tehom 72–3, 75
Mötsnik, Harri 10
Murdoch, Iris: *The Sea, the Sea* 72
music:
  Brahms 18, 60
  Haydn's *Creation* 31
  sustains Estonian faith 7–9
myth and story:
  Babylonian 17, 31
  Biblical 19
  Poseidon 19
  see also Biblical images and stories

nature:
  faith-sustaining 12–13
  life-changing forces 44–5
Nicodemus: puzzled by birth 102–3
Noah 33–5: *see also* Flood
Nod/the Land of Wandering 51

Oengo, Hugo 6–7
Orthodox Church, Estonia 3
Otto, Rudolph 53

Pärnamets, Olav 6
Pärt, Arvo 8
St Paul:
  authority and power 89–90
  blinded by the light 53
  struggle with sin 110
  tehom/the deep 43
Paul, Toomas 4

St Peter 71:
baptism 114–15
recognition of Christ 78
spirits in prison 95, 96
Pettersson, Per 25, 67
Philippians, Letter to 90
Psalms, Book of:
confusion of deep waters 46
creation 38
deliverance 124–5
the desert 48–9, 50
God in the depths 40
liberation 98
pit imagery 54–7
self-acceptance 112
tears 46

redemption: God's plan 89–90
Revelation, Book of 131–2:
kosmos 70
slaying monsters 84–6
spirits 74
Roman Catholic Church:
controversies 64
Romans, Letter to 43:
children 111–12
creation 103, 117
struggle with sin 110
Rummo, Paul-Eerik 9
Russalka (ferry) 13, 19

Saag, Ewald 4
Salumaa, Elmar 4
Satan:
becomes 'the devil' 79
defining 79–80
demons 82–4
dualism of good and evil 60, 80–2
Gerasene demons 82–4
as God's agent 76–7
temptation of Jesus 78–9
Schofield, Charles: *Annotated Bible* 65
seas and oceans:
Exodus parting of the water 38–9
Hebrew *tehom* 29, 30–2
mystery 21–3
symbol of evil 23
Sibelius, Jean 18
Silvia, Queen of Sweden 25
Sisask, Urmas 9
Song of Songs 87
Soviet Union:
Domination System 70
repression in Estonia 2–7
Sweden:
effect of *Estonia* sinking 24–5
religious education restored 67

Tartu University 4
tehom/the deep 42:
baptism 91, 113–15
crucifixion and descent into hell 93
defined 29, 30–2
embracing 130–2
evil 82–3
God's protection from 81
God's purpose 119–21
life-changing possibilities 123–4
many images 55
monsters 72–3, 75
rescue and renewal 124–5
revelation and discovery 125–6

tehom/the deep (*cont.*)
taming the waters 46–7
validity for all time 118–19
vision in Revelation 85
Temple, Archbishop William 73
Theological Institute, Tallinn 4
Tillich, Paul: *Shaking of the Foundations* 58–9
time 88–9
Titanic (film) 26–7
Titanic (ship): parable of 26–8
Tobias, Rudolf 7
tohu wa-bohu/formless void 30–1, 45, 87
tombs: and the womb 104
Tormis, Veljo 9

Viljari, Ago 4

war and conflict: disillusionment 66
water:
baptism 113–15, 116, 130
challenge of the deep 20–1
imagery 15–18
personality of the sea 18–20
resources 22–3
taming the early chaos 45–7
tears 46
Wink, Walter:
Domination System 68–9
on the Legion 84
Unmasking the Powers 76
Wright, Tom 89

The Society for Promoting Christian Knowledge (SPCK) has as its purpose three main tasks:

- **Communicating the Christian faith in its rich diversity**
- **Helping people to understand the Christian faith and to develop their personal faith**
- **Equipping Christians for mission and ministry**

SPCK Worldwide serves the Church through Christian literature and communication projects in over 100 countries. Special schemes also provide books for those training for ministry in many parts of the developing world. SPCK Worldwide's ministry involves Churches of many traditions. This worldwide service depends upon the generosity of others and all gifts are spent wholly on ministry programmes, without deductions.

SPCK Bookshops support the life of the Christian community by making available a full range of Christian literature and other resources, and by providing support to bookstalls and book agents throughout the UK. SPCK Bookshops' mail order department meets the needs of overseas customers and those unable to have access to local bookshops.

SPCK Publishing produces Christian books and resources, covering a wide range of inspirational, pastoral, practical and academic subjects. Authors are drawn from many different Christian traditions, and publications aim to meet the needs of a wide variety of readers in the UK and throughout the world.

The Society does not necessarily endorse the individual views contained in its publications, but hopes they stimulate readers to think about and further develop their Christian faith.

For further information about the Society, please write to:
SPCK, Holy Trinity Church, Marylebone Road,
London NW1 4DU, United Kingdom.
Telephone: 0171 387 5282